Don't You ?

Miss Mensa's Theory on the Case
of Christopher Watts

Brenda Irish Heintzelman

MISS MENSA'S THEORY ~ on the Case of Christopher Watts Specific to Family Violence and Child Abuse is an opinion essay written to explore whether Christopher Watts is guilty of murdering his wife and their daughters beyond all reasonable doubt.

Copyright@2019 All rights reserved.

Butterfly Publishing, Traverse City, MI

Copyright@2019 All rights reserved. No reprints, duplicates, or electronic transfer in violation of U.S. copyright law is allowed, in whole or in part, in any way, shape, form, or fashion, for any purpose, without written permission from the author who can be reached at missmensa@gmail.com.

MISS MENSA'S THEORY ~ on the Case of Christopher Watts Specific to Family Violence and Child Abuse is an opinion essay written to explore whether Christopher Watts is guilty of murdering his wife and their daughters beyond all reasonable doubt.

MISS MENSA'S THEORY ~ on the Case of Christopher Watts Specific to Family Violence and Child Abuse is an opinion essay written to explore whether Christopher Watts is guilty of murdering his wife and their daughters beyond all reasonable doubt.

MISS MENSA'S THEORY ~ on the Case of Christopher Watts Specific to Family Violence and Child Abuse is an opinion essay written to explore whether Christopher Watts is guilty of murdering his wife and their daughters beyond all reasonable doubt.

This book is dedicated to Bella and Ce Ce Watts ~ two innocent children who were murdered by one of their parents in what should have been the safety of their own home.

MISS MENSA'S THEORY ~ on the Case of Christopher Watts Specific to Family Violence and Child Abuse is an opinion essay written to explore whether Christopher Watts is guilty of murdering his wife and their daughters beyond all reasonable doubt.

MISS MENSA'S THEORY ~ on the Case of Christopher Watts Specific to Family Violence and Child Abuse is an opinion essay written to explore whether Christopher Watts is guilty of murdering his wife and their daughters beyond all reasonable doubt.

"Violators cannot live with the truth: survivors cannot live without it. There are those who still, once again, are poised to invalidate and deny us. If we don't assert our truth, it may again be relegated to fantasy.

But the truth won't go away. It will keep surfacing until it is recognized. Truth will outlast any campaigns mounted against it, no matter how mighty, clever, or long.

It is invincible."

-- Chrystine Oksana

MISS MENSA'S THEORY ~ on the Case of Christopher Watts Specific to Family Violence and Child Abuse is an opinion essay written to explore whether Christopher Watts is guilty of murdering his wife and their daughters beyond all reasonable doubt.

MISS MENSA'S THEORY ~ on the Case of Christopher Watts Specific to Family Violence and Child Abuse is an opinion essay written to explore whether Christopher Watts is guilty of murdering his wife and their daughters beyond all reasonable doubt.

"The Way to Right Wrongs is to Turn the Light of Truth Upon Them."
--Ida B. Wells-Barnett

MISS MENSA'S THEORY ~ on the Case of Christopher Watts Specific to Family Violence and Child Abuse is an opinion essay written to explore whether Christopher Watts is guilty of murdering his wife and their daughters beyond all reasonable doubt.

MISS MENSA'S THEORY ~ on the Case of Christopher Watts Specific to Family Violence and Child Abuse is an opinion essay written to explore whether Christopher Watts is guilty of murdering his wife and their daughters beyond all reasonable doubt.

"There is nothing that is going to make people hate you more,

and love you more,

than telling the truth."

— Stefan Molyneux

MISS MENSA'S THEORY ~ on the Case of Christopher Watts Specific to Family Violence and Child Abuse is an opinion essay written to explore whether Christopher Watts is guilty of murdering his wife and their daughters beyond all reasonable doubt.

MISS MENSA'S THEORY ~ on the Case of Christopher Watts Specific to Family Violence and Child Abuse is an opinion essay written to explore whether Christopher Watts is guilty of murdering his wife and their daughters beyond all reasonable doubt.

Don't You Save Her!

Miss Mensa's Theory on the Case of Christopher Watts

MISS MENSA'S THEORY ~ on the Case of Christopher Watts Specific to Family Violence and Child Abuse is an opinion essay written to explore whether Christopher Watts is guilty of murdering his wife and their daughters beyond all reasonable doubt.

MISS MENSA'S THEORY ~ on the Case of Christopher Watts Specific to Family Violence and Child Abuse is an opinion essay written to explore whether Christopher Watts is guilty of murdering his wife and their daughters beyond all reasonable doubt.

DON'T YOU SAVE HER!

Miss Mensa's Theory

The Case of Christopher Watts

Foreword

Lighting the Path

The Timeline

"Health Challenges"

Isolation from Family and Friends

Was Christopher Watts a Battered Husband?

Financial Abuse

Munchausen by Proxy

Was There an Open CPS Case?

Her OTHER TWO DAUGHTERS?

Were her LIES about to be EXPOSED?

Happy Birthday

Was Christopher Watts Telling the Truth When He Said HE DID NOT MURDER HIS CHILDREN?

Afterword

About the Author

MISS MENSA'S THEORY ~ on the Case of Christopher Watts Specific to Family Violence and Child Abuse is an opinion essay written to explore whether Christopher Watts is guilty of murdering his wife and their daughters beyond all reasonable doubt.

MISS MENSA'S THEORY ~ on the Case of Christopher Watts Specific to Family Violence and Child Abuse is an opinion essay written to explore whether Christopher Watts is guilty of murdering his wife and their daughters beyond all reasonable doubt.

Foreword

When a criminal case hits the headline news, the parties to the case enter onto what is known as the PUBLIC STAGE. In the U.S. we have the freedom to discuss these cases, including the behavior and actions of the parties involved.

Except, it seems, in the case of Christopher Watts.

For over ten years straight, I have enjoyed discussing and writing about true crime cases that are in the headline news.

Until the case of Christopher Watts came along.

And within two weeks, all hell broke loose.

It soon became obvious there was an organized group of gangstalking thugs in position to attack innocent people on social media – for simply discussing this case.

MISS MENSA'S THEORY ~ on the Case of Christopher Watts Specific to Family Violence and Child Abuse is an opinion essay written to explore whether Christopher Watts is guilty of murdering his wife and their daughters beyond all reasonable doubt.

I have been getting attacked by this organized group of gangstalking thugs from social media who claim they are "paid online investigators" and "professional computer hacks" for over thirteen months straight.

They have created and posted literally hundreds of videos and thousands of comments all over the internet – attacking my YouTube channel name "Miss Mensa" and attacking me both personally and professionally too.

They create false internet posts then read them off in their videos claiming it's PUBLIC INFORMATION.

It isn't.

And they know it.

What they are doing is in clear violation of multiple civil and criminal laws.

Recently, one of their own was sentenced to serve two years' probation. She was one of the

MISS MENSA'S THEORY ~ on the Case of Christopher Watts Specific to Family Violence and Child Abuse is an opinion essay written to explore whether Christopher Watts is guilty of murdering his wife and their daughters beyond all reasonable doubt.

attackers who had a job – most of them publicly discuss being on the government dole. And as a result of her online criminal activities, she lost the job that she had held for eight years straight.

At her sentencing hearing last week she stood there crying while her lawyer read her statement to the court – that she was sorry – that she didn't realize that what she was taking part in was wrong – that there is a "pact" among women who are actively attacking and threatening innocent people online – people they are directed to attack – for simply discussing the case of Christopher Watts.

This woman and her co-horts are not the only "pact" of attackers – there are plenty more – teams of people who make it their daily mission to harm and to threaten innocent people online and in real-life too - as they make phone calls to our family members and friends, and to our

MISS MENSA'S THEORY ~ on the Case of Christopher Watts Specific to Family Violence and Child Abuse is an opinion essay written to explore whether Christopher Watts is guilty of murdering his wife and their daughters beyond all reasonable doubt.

employers, and they file false police reports against us - claiming that we're the ones who are harassing them.

The attackers have harassed, stalked, bullied, and threatened me publicly since September 3, 2018, just two weeks after the case of Christopher Watts hit the headline news.

They claim they have the right to say whatever they want to say about me because I'm an author.

They don't.

Yes, I am an author. But being an author does not allow a group of scumbag thugs to dox, threaten, and harass me for thirteen months straight.

In fact, they are criminals who are vulnerable to being arrested for the many crimes they have committed and that they are continuing to commit against me, including harassing telephone calls, online harassment, stalking, bullying, and threats.

MISS MENSA'S THEORY ~ on the Case of Christopher Watts Specific to Family Violence and Child Abuse is an opinion essay written to explore whether Christopher Watts is guilty of murdering his wife and their daughters beyond all reasonable doubt.

They are also liable for damages stemming from the civil infractions they have committed and are continuing to commit against me - including defamation, slander, libel, and intentional infliction of emotional distress.

There are "online reputation management" (ORM) companies involved in the attacks too.

The ORM companies swoop in to offer to "help repair" my online "reputation" – the fees start at 300 dollars per month per post – and they don't promise to remove the libelous and harassing post either. They offer to try to help "demote" ONE POST further down in the search results.

This isn't a one-time fee for "helping" with just one post – they want a contract signed with a minimum commitment of "four to five months". That's $1,500 to "help" with just ONE post – while there are, by now, in just the last year – literally thousands of libelous posts which have been created and posted by the online thugs.

MISS MENSA'S THEORY ~ on the Case of Christopher Watts Specific to Family Violence and Child Abuse is an opinion essay written to explore whether Christopher Watts is guilty of murdering his wife and their daughters beyond all reasonable doubt.

This is nothing short of an all-out scam that is being perpetrated against thousands of innocent people each day. And online platforms such as YouTube and Facebook are not only allowing it to happen, they are encouraging the attacks to continue against us by virtue of their permission for their platforms to be used for the attacks.

Online platforms like YouTube and Facebook could easily remove the attackers' threatening and harassing posts. But they do nothing. While hiding behind their "community standards" to "show" they care, in fact, they DO NOT expect the attackers to adhere to any standard at all.

Just follow the money – while the attackers create the fake posts to harm us, then "online reputation management" companies swoop in FOR A FEE to "help" us repair the damage to our reputations they have caused, some of the online reputation management companies claim they

---

MISS MENSA'S THEORY ~ on the Case of Christopher Watts Specific to Family Violence and Child Abuse is an opinion essay written to explore whether Christopher Watts is guilty of murdering his wife and their daughters beyond all reasonable doubt.

actually pay the online platforms a percentage of the fees they collect.

So, according to the ORMs, the platforms which are allowing the attacks to occur in the first place are being paid a percentage of what the ORMs are raking in? If this is true then it appears there's a lot of money flowing in - at the expense of decent people who in no way deserve to be attacked by the online gangstalking thugs.

Specific to the discussion of the case of Christopher Watts - as the gangstalking thugs attempt to control the narrative on social media - their goal appears to be to somehow rewrite the reputation of Christopher Watts' wife - BY ATTEMPTING TO "DESTROY" MINE.

Their abusive tactics are clear - use Miss Mensa as the scapegoat to show people what might happen to them if they dare to openly discuss this case.

MISS MENSA'S THEORY ~ on the Case of Christopher Watts Specific to Family Violence and Child Abuse is an opinion essay written to explore whether Christopher Watts is guilty of murdering his wife and their daughters beyond all reasonable doubt.

The attackers have warned me that I am ALLOWED to discuss any true crime case that I want to discuss - EXCEPT the case of Christopher Watts.

Recently the attackers claimed they were able to shut down my true crime case discussion channel on YouTube by "mass reporting" it as hate speech. YouTube had already manually reviewed each video for monetization and did not find any hate speech, of course. But when a group of gangstalking thugs "mass report" it's clear that YouTube doesn't care about video content - instead it appears YouTube cares about keeping the "online reputations management" companies rolling in the money.

So, I started my new channel on Bitchute - where they DO NOT ALLOW harassment - and I started posting my videos to Patreon too.

My reason for writing this book is simple - because there are literally thousands of us

MISS MENSA'S THEORY ~ on the Case of Christopher Watts Specific to Family Violence and Child Abuse is an opinion essay written to explore whether Christopher Watts is guilty of murdering his wife and their daughters beyond all reasonable doubt.

discussing the case whose interest has been piqued, first stemming from the attacks against us, and then by the details emerging about the case itself which do not fit the narrative being promoted by the attackers from the start.

We deserve to be able to discuss this case like we discuss every other true crime case in the news – with or without permission from the gangstalking thugs.

We're asking questions.

Because we want answers.

Why is there an organized effort to control the narrative on the case of Christopher Watts?

What is it the attackers were hired to hide?

Is it true that Christopher Watts' wife was Bipolar - as her father-in-law suggested during his interview?

Is it true that she was medically abusing their children - as we've been told by people who claim

MISS MENSA'S THEORY ~ on the Case of Christopher Watts Specific to Family Violence and Child Abuse is an opinion essay written to explore whether Christopher Watts is guilty of murdering his wife and their daughters beyond all reasonable doubt.

to know that she was caught by the hospital in December of 2016?

Is it true that she was a con? Is it true that at the time of her death there was an open CPS case against her? If so, is it true that she was not allowed to be alone with their children?

Is it true that Christopher Watts was a battered husband?

Be clear, we have the right to discuss true crime cases that are on the public stage – without being attacked.

Yet, the attackers have "mass reported" and shut down discussion channels and groups to interfere with our right to discuss true crime cases on social media. The attackers are also flooding my book reviews with fake posts. They don't bother to read my work. They don't bother to discuss the cases. Instead, they post libelous comments accusing me of cheating on my ex? Accusing me of lying about my law degree? Accusing me of lying

MISS MENSA'S THEORY ~ on the Case of Christopher Watts Specific to Family Violence and Child Abuse is an opinion essay written to explore whether Christopher Watts is guilty of murdering his wife and their daughters beyond all reasonable doubt.

about having my own real estate company? Also, the attackers claim that I plagiarize my work. Obviously they don't even know the meaning of the word.

Clearly, those who are attempting to silence us richly deserve to be arrested and jailed for the bad acts they have committed and continue to commit against us.

Because we have the right to speak. We have the right to discuss true crime cases that are on the public stage. We have the right to ask questions and to state our opinions on the case while the people who are attempting to silence us – lose their right to freely speak the second they use free speech to harass and harm us.

There are two little girls - Bella and Ce Ce Watts - at the center of this case who deserve for us to continue the discussion. Because Bella and Ce Ce DESERVE FOR THE TRUTH TO BE KNOWN.

MISS MENSA'S THEORY ~ on the Case of Christopher Watts Specific to Family Violence and Child Abuse is an opinion essay written to explore whether Christopher Watts is guilty of murdering his wife and their daughters beyond all reasonable doubt.

Is it possible their father was telling the truth in his first police interview when he insisted that HE DID NOT MURDER HIS CHILDREN?

Join the discussion.

And YOU decide.

MISS MENSA'S THEORY ~ on the Case of Christopher Watts Specific to Family Violence and Child Abuse is an opinion essay written to explore whether Christopher Watts is guilty of murdering his wife and their daughters beyond all reasonable doubt.

Lighting the Path

When the case of Christopher Watts first hit the headline news back on August 13, 2018, the public was told that his "missing" wife from Colorado was a high-level employee of a multi-billion-dollar multi-level marketing company who had "retired" from nursing to become a stay-at-home mom.

We were told she was highly successful. We were told she was last seen just hours before when one of her associates dropped her off at home following a "business trip" to Arizona over the weekend.

We were told she was diabetic. We were told she had fibromyalgia, lupus, and a long list of other

MISS MENSA'S THEORY ~ on the Case of Christopher Watts Specific to Family Violence and Child Abuse is an opinion essay written to explore whether Christopher Watts is guilty of murdering his wife and their daughters beyond all reasonable doubt.

ailments and diseases too which she had somehow magically overcome because she was so determined, and so amazing, and so gifted that she set her highly intelligent mind on overcoming her "health challenges".

Well, guess what folks, we were being lied to. Right from the start.

Christopher Watts' wife was never a successful employee of any MLM. And she was never a nurse either.

And while it may very well be that she was a "stay-at-home mom" as the official narrative claims, the TRUTH is that while she was staying at home - both preschool age children were in daycare.

Her "health challenges" and especially her miracle cures really need a book of their own. Because the list of her SELF-PROCLAIMED illnesses and diseases really is that long.

MISS MENSA'S THEORY ~ on the Case of Christopher Watts Specific to Family Violence and Child Abuse is an opinion essay written to explore whether Christopher Watts is guilty of murdering his wife and their daughters beyond all reasonable doubt.

And evidently, so is her list of lies.

Suffice it to say, I don't believe she had any PHYSCIAL "health challenges" at all.

That's right.

I said it.

I believe that all the hooey about her having Lupus, or Fibromyalgia, or Endometriosis, or Diabetes, or Celiac Disease, or any of the other diseases she claimed to have was all just a bunch of hogwash.

I think she used her supposed ailments to gain attention and control.

To con people.

To get her own way.

Within two weeks of this case hitting the headlines, innocent people who were discussing the case of Christopher Watts on social media were targeted to be attacked.

MISS MENSA'S THEORY ~ on the Case of Christopher Watts Specific to Family Violence and Child Abuse is an opinion essay written to explore whether Christopher Watts is guilty of murdering his wife and their daughters beyond all reasonable doubt.

Including me.

The attackers accused us of having filed multiple bankruptcies, of being divorced, of lying about our careers and education, and they called us child abusers too.

So, those of us who were under attack got together and compared notes. There were just a couple who had ever filed a bankruptcy, and they had each filed just one time. There were a few of us who were divorced but the majority of those of us under attack were not. We had solid careers, with some of us owning our own businesses. Most of us were college graduates too - with three of us also holding post graduate degrees.

NOT ONE OF US who were being attacked by the gangstalking thugs has EVER abused a child.

So, we got to talking and we wondered out loud if maybe these are the areas of Christopher Watts'

MISS MENSA'S THEORY ~ on the Case of Christopher Watts Specific to Family Violence and Child Abuse is an opinion essay written to explore whether Christopher Watts is guilty of murdering his wife and their daughters beyond all reasonable doubt.

wife's "reputation" which the attackers were hired to hide.

We dug in.

And this is what we found.

Multiple bankruptcies?

Christopher Watts' wife filed for bankruptcy in 2015.

Divorced?

Christopher Watts' wife was divorced prior to meeting him.

Lying about our careers?

Christopher Watts' wife was not a high-level employee of any multi-level marketing company. And she was NEVER a nurse.

Lying about our education?

Christopher Watts' wife was not a college graduate.

Child abusers?

MISS MENSA'S THEORY ~ on the Case of Christopher Watts Specific to Family Violence and Child Abuse is an opinion essay written to explore whether Christopher Watts is guilty of murdering his wife and their daughters beyond all reasonable doubt.

Well, from what we have learned so far from the boatload of information about the case that was released to the public, those of us who are under attack agree it is quite likely, and reasonable to believe, that in fact, Christopher Watts' wife was medically abusing their children. It's called Munchausen by Proxy which is one of the most dangerous forms of child abuse of all.

From the moment the attacks against us started, it seemed the attackers have been lighting the path for us, through their false accusations, to exactly what it is they do not want us to see about Christopher Watts' wife.

And it gets worse.

A lot worse.

The attackers claim we are psycho. Seriously psycho. As in severely mentally ill. As in Bipolar, Narcissistic, and Schizophrenic too. We've heard it all.

MISS MENSA'S THEORY ~ on the Case of Christopher Watts Specific to Family Violence and Child Abuse is an opinion essay written to explore whether Christopher Watts is guilty of murdering his wife and their daughters beyond all reasonable doubt.

And each time they attack us by telling others we are in need of immediate psychiatric care, those of us they are attacking dig deeper into the case details for any evidence that in fact Christopher Watts' wife may have actually been suffering from severe mental illness at the time of her death.

The attackers are also well-versed in the issue of suicide - telling us to hurry up and die while telling others that we are suicidal.

So we dug further into the details of the case and we wondered, could it be true, could it be that the attackers are lighting the path for us once again, as they have from the start, without intending to show us exactly what it is they are seemingly so hell-bent on trying to hide?

Could it be that Christopher Watts' wife was mentally ill? Could it also be that Christopher Watts' wife was suicidal?

MISS MENSA'S THEORY ~ on the Case of Christopher Watts Specific to Family Violence and Child Abuse is an opinion essay written to explore whether Christopher Watts is guilty of murdering his wife and their daughters beyond all reasonable doubt.

Could it be that Christopher Watts' wife murdered their daughters and then killed herself?

The attackers are now accusing us of having had children who we abandoned for others to raise.

And we wonder...

MISS MENSA'S THEORY ~ on the Case of Christopher Watts Specific to Family Violence and Child Abuse is an opinion essay written to explore whether Christopher Watts is guilty of murdering his wife and their daughters beyond all reasonable doubt.

Miss Mensa's Timeline Series

The most popular videos I uploaded to the Miss Mensa channel on YouTube was the Ten-part Timeline Series, which is now available for you to view on Bitchute.com. I will informally outline the first five videos for you here which run from December of 2009 when she magically qualified for a mortgage with a down payment of less than 10% - through 2012, after they moved when Christopher Watts' wife claimed that "the weather in Colorado helped 95% of her diseases".

In addition to joining the discussion on true crime cases on Bitchute.com, you can also join us on Facebook at "Discuss True Crime with Miss Mensa".

MISS MENSA'S THEORY ~ on the Case of Christopher Watts Specific to Family Violence and Child Abuse is an opinion essay written to explore whether Christopher Watts is guilty of murdering his wife and their daughters beyond all reasonable doubt.

Timeline Series Video #1

I've been contacted by people who claim Christopher Watts' wife was not allowed to be alone with their children. I encourage the people who are calling me to also contact law enforcement with any information they may have on the case.

THE TRUTH HAS THE RIGHT TO BE KNOWN, BECAUSE IN MY OPINION, BELLA AND CELESTE DESERVE TO HAVE THE TRUTH OF WHAT THEY SUFFERED THROUGH TO BE KNOWN.

Christopher Watts' wife started her Facebook profile in 2007.

And she barely posted any comments at all for the next three years.

December 2009 – she bought a house (magically) with less than 10% down payment.

January of 2010 – accusations of embezzlement?

MISS MENSA'S THEORY ~ on the Case of Christopher Watts Specific to Family Violence and Child Abuse is an opinion essay written to explore whether Christopher Watts is guilty of murdering his wife and their daughters beyond all reasonable doubt.

Many years later, she would claim that in the first week of May of 2010 she was diagnosed with three serious diseases all in the same week. Yet, she never mentioned her alleged illnesses around that time at all on social media. She was posting a lot. But not at all about having been diagnosed with three major diseases all in one week.

Over the summer, she posted a series of "escaping" posts. Example – she wanted a one-way ticket to away from anyone who knew her.

August 10, 2010 – her first date with Christopher Watts.

After meeting Christopher Watts, she suddenly starts posting all about Lupus.

Pain, fatigue, migraines, memory loss, hair loss, posts were posted AFTER meeting Christopher Watts.

Also, she started posting about medical testing – an M.R.I, blood work, another M.R.I, a

MISS MENSA'S THEORY ~ on the Case of Christopher Watts Specific to Family Violence and Child Abuse is an opinion essay written to explore whether Christopher Watts is guilty of murdering his wife and their daughters beyond all reasonable doubt.

colonoscopy, etc. yet she NEVER mentions A.N.A. (the test for Lupus).

She claimed she was leading Lupus fundraiser walks and in some of her posts she advised people to donate straight to her.

She made T-shirts about Lupus and was selling them privately. She held a yard sale for Lupus. And she held a raffle for Lupus too, claiming that ALL the proceeds would be donated to the Lupus Foundation, of course.

Interesting that she never mentioned her migraines or fatigue or feeling ill at all until AFTER she met Christopher Watts.

Timeline Series #2

After meeting Christopher Watts, she starts talking about her supposed diseases.

One month later, she leads a Lupus fundraiser walk.

MISS MENSA'S THEORY ~ on the Case of Christopher Watts Specific to Family Violence and Child Abuse is an opinion essay written to explore whether Christopher Watts is guilty of murdering his wife and their daughters beyond all reasonable doubt.

Starts posting ad nauseum about medical testing AFTER meeting Christopher Watts but NEVER mentions the test for Lupus.

August 10, 2010 first date.

Three weeks later she started posting about having Lupus.

And she quit her job.

Remember, she had a mortgage to pay. So, who was paying the mortgage payments?

She claimed she quit her job due to her illnesses and diseases.

In later posts, she said that ever since she quit her job that her diseases were in "constant flare".

She put an ad on care.com in November of 2010 to try to find a babysitting job.

She claimed she was also working part-time for the Guess clothing store.

MISS MENSA'S THEORY ~ on the Case of Christopher Watts Specific to Family Violence and Child Abuse is an opinion essay written to explore whether Christopher Watts is guilty of murdering his wife and their daughters beyond all reasonable doubt.

She quit her full-time job in August and started babysitting in November. But the family she was babysitting for moved to Colorado in February of 2011.

She then returned to the job she had quit in August.

In June of 2011, she announced that she was going to become a nurse.

(The woman she babysat for was a nurse).

She claims she has been accepted into the Presbyterian School of Nursing.

August 10, 2011 – they spend the day at the beach (even though she claimed she couldn't handle humidity) and they become engaged.

August 2011 – she commented that she wanted to move to Colorado.

September 2011 – she announces that she was accepted into the nursing program and would be starting in January 2012. This is confusing since

MISS MENSA'S THEORY ~ on the Case of Christopher Watts Specific to Family Violence and Child Abuse is an opinion essay written to explore whether Christopher Watts is guilty of murdering his wife and their daughters beyond all reasonable doubt.

she had previously posted that she was already accepted into the program.

November 2011 – they travel to Colorado and visited with the woman who she used to babysit for. After that trip she commented they would be back to Colorado sooner than they think.

December of 2011 – bridal shower.

December 2011 – while she has already claimed she was going to be working full-time and attending the nursing program full-time, in fact, she quit her job again before the alleged nursing program started.

January 2012 – she claims she starts the nursing program.

February 2012 – she claims she has been diagnosed with Celiac disease.

April 2012 – She claims she lost her insurance.

MISS MENSA'S THEORY ~ on the Case of Christopher Watts Specific to Family Violence and Child Abuse is an opinion essay written to explore whether Christopher Watts is guilty of murdering his wife and their daughters beyond all reasonable doubt.

Timeline Series #3

Recap on the nursing school claim –

June 2011 – she announces she wants to become a nurse.

She says she took the exam and that she started the nursing assistant program. She said she would have the results of the exam in September. But in September she doesn't mention anything about any exam results.

In December, she claims she was accepted into the program.

In January, she claims she started the nursing program.

She also claimed her house was broken into.

February 2012 – Christopher Watts moved to Colorado.

February 2012 – she claimed that she was diagnosed with Celiac disease.

MISS MENSA'S THEORY ~ on the Case of Christopher Watts Specific to Family Violence and Child Abuse is an opinion essay written to explore whether Christopher Watts is guilty of murdering his wife and their daughters beyond all reasonable doubt.

In April of 2012 – she moved to Colorado before putting her house on the market. So, there goes the idea of nursing school.

Note – in one of her videos she said that she did attend college but that she dropped out to support her ex-husband. She said that she went back to school eventually but her "conditions" made it too hard for her to complete the program.

She claimed that after moving in April of 2012 that the weather in Colorado helped 95% of her diseases.

When Christopher Watts spoke with the police in August of 2018, he told them she had Lupus and Rosacea with no mention of any other diseases.

He also told the police she was off all her meds when she got to Colorado.

Was she even on any meds in the first place?

MISS MENSA'S THEORY ~ on the Case of Christopher Watts Specific to Family Violence and Child Abuse is an opinion essay written to explore whether Christopher Watts is guilty of murdering his wife and their daughters beyond all reasonable doubt.

I contacted the nursing school and was unable to confirm that the "accelerated program" she claimed she was accepted into ever existed.

She couldn't even pronounce "shin splints" so I highly doubt she was ever accepted into any nursing program.

I think she was telling Christopher Watts whatever she figured that he may want to hear.

I think she told a lot of stories. And I think Christopher Watts believed them all.

Timeline Series #4

Again, encouraging people who have been contacting me with information about this case to pick up their phones and call law enforcement with what they know.

Series of posts claiming how busy she is and how busy she will be – she claims she will be taking a

MISS MENSA'S THEORY ~ on the Case of Christopher Watts Specific to Family Violence and Child Abuse is an opinion essay written to explore whether Christopher Watts is guilty of murdering his wife and their daughters beyond all reasonable doubt.

nursing program that will accomplish four years in two in what she calls an Associate in Science program.

January 10, 2012 – heading to class.

January 10, 2012 – she laments about dealing with Lupus and Fibromyalgia while going to school full-time.

January 2012 – she says that planning a wedding all by herself "kinda sucks" while she's a full-time nursing student too.

She claims that her first term is "like double the work of A and P. It is crazy. I hate science and I am looking for a tutor for me to just stay ahead because I already feel lost. It's just A and P that I am not grabbing".

January 25, 2012 – her house was broken into. She claims she was in the house while the intruders were still there.

MISS MENSA'S THEORY ~ on the Case of Christopher Watts Specific to Family Violence and Child Abuse is an opinion essay written to explore whether Christopher Watts is guilty of murdering his wife and their daughters beyond all reasonable doubt.

Texting during class and one of her friends said to pay attention to the teacher. She was talking about another student – she calls the other student freaky and weird and says that the other student stinks.

February 9, 2012 – announces she has Celiac disease.

April 24, 2012 – "I did not take my test early because I wanted to see you guys again" – posted in response to a student who said it was her last day of classes.

Nursing school programs in 2011 and 2012 were raising their GPA requirements to get the very best applicants possible due to the stiff competition at the time to get into a nursing school.

ASN?

She claimed she was going to be an R.N. in two years, with a four-year degree. But she was

MISS MENSA'S THEORY ~ on the Case of Christopher Watts Specific to Family Violence and Child Abuse is an opinion essay written to explore whether Christopher Watts is guilty of murdering his wife and their daughters beyond all reasonable doubt.

claiming she would have an "ASN" degree which is not a four-year degree.

The school she claimed she was attending does not list an associate degree program. The school offers the BSN and the MSN programs.

Checking specifically for the year 2011 – I found the Peterson book which lists the nursing programs offered in that year. On page 322, it shows the school she claimed she was attending. The degrees the school offered that year were a BSN and an MSN. I think that Christopher Watts' wife was lying about being accepted into any nursing program.

Timeline Series #5

In my opinion, Christopher Watts was conned from the start. I do not believe that his wife was honest, and I don't believe she had good

MISS MENSA'S THEORY ~ on the Case of Christopher Watts Specific to Family Violence and Child Abuse is an opinion essay written to explore whether Christopher Watts is guilty of murdering his wife and their daughters beyond all reasonable doubt.

intentions at all – when she met him – throughout their marriage – and including the night she died.

Note the phone number and name of the CPS worker in the discovery documents. I do think that she was medically abusing poor little Bella and Ce Ce. I do think there was an open CPS case against her.

I do believe that she was a con. And I believe that Christopher Watts believed whatever she told him.

December of 2011 – following three car break-ins at her place of employment she quit her job again.

January 2012 – she says she started attending a nursing program. However, the degree she claimed she was earning doesn't appear to have been offered at the school she claimed she was attending.

January 25, 2012 – she claimed "so, I go into master bedroom. Found door open! They were still

MISS MENSA'S THEORY ~ on the Case of Christopher Watts Specific to Family Violence and Child Abuse is an opinion essay written to explore whether Christopher Watts is guilty of murdering his wife and their daughters beyond all reasonable doubt.

in the house. OMG scary! Why is 2012 so mean to me?"

She says that Lupus and school don't allow her much spending money.

February 2012 – Christopher Watts moved to Colorado. He would later say that her doctor told her that she had to move to Colorado for her health. Yet, the only meds she was on were for her migraines.

She moved to Colorado in April.

In May, she put the house on the market, and it sold in September. She would later claim she made a profit. But she didn't. After paying closing costs, she probably lost many thousands of dollars on the deal.

In July, she started working at the same car dealership where Christopher Watts started working when he moved to Colorado in February.

MISS MENSA'S THEORY ~ on the Case of Christopher Watts Specific to Family Violence and Child Abuse is an opinion essay written to explore whether Christopher Watts is guilty of murdering his wife and their daughters beyond all reasonable doubt.

So, what have we learned so far? Well, to me it appears that Christopher Watts' wife was conning him right from the start of their relationship.

She bought a house in December of 2009.

Really?

With whose money?

How on earth did she qualify for that mortgage? Remember, she worked right in the office of that auto parts store, right? Gee, I wonder who filled out the "income verification form" when it was mailed to the employer by the lender.

In January 2010, just one month after magically qualifying for that mortgage, rumors began circulating through town that she was involved in some sort of financial mismanagement accusations. Could those rumors have stemmed from the lawsuits filed the previous year which named her as one of the defendants?

MISS MENSA'S THEORY ~ on the Case of Christopher Watts Specific to Family Violence and Child Abuse is an opinion essay written to explore whether Christopher Watts is guilty of murdering his wife and their daughters beyond all reasonable doubt.

We learned that before meeting Christopher Watts she failed to mention any diseases and then within one month of their first date on August 10, 2010 she started posting ad nauseum about her Lupus, Fibro, and Sjogren's and how terribly sick she felt a lot of the time.

She also quit her job within one month of their first date.

Then in November, she started babysitting one child for a family that moved away in February of 2011 when the mother got a nursing position in Colorado.

In June of 2011, she posted for the first time that she wanted to be a nurse.

Another miracle occurred in December of 2011 when she posted that she was accepted into a highly respected nursing program.

Except we have been unable to find any proof of her claim that the program she said she was

MISS MENSA'S THEORY ~ on the Case of Christopher Watts Specific to Family Violence and Child Abuse is an opinion essay written to explore whether Christopher Watts is guilty of murdering his wife and their daughters beyond all reasonable doubt.

accepted into was even offered in 2011 at that school.

In February of 2012, Christopher Watts moved to Colorado after being told by his then fiancé that her doctor told her she needed to move to Colorado for her health challenges.

In April of 2012, after claiming she completed her first term in that nursing program that she claimed she was attending, she moved to Colorado.

In July of 2012, she was hired by the same car dealership where Christopher Watts was employed.

I don't believe that she was ever accepted into any nursing program.

And I don't believe she had any of the physical "health challenges" she claimed to have either. As I previously stated, I think she used fake

---

MISS MENSA'S THEORY ~ on the Case of Christopher Watts Specific to Family Violence and Child Abuse is an opinion essay written to explore whether Christopher Watts is guilty of murdering his wife and their daughters beyond all reasonable doubt.

illnesses in order to get attention and to maintain control.

Now, let's take a good look at those "health challenges" she claimed to have.

MISS MENSA'S THEORY ~ on the Case of Christopher Watts Specific to Family Violence and Child Abuse is an opinion essay written to explore whether Christopher Watts is guilty of murdering his wife and their daughters beyond all reasonable doubt.

"Health Challenges"

She claimed that she was diagnosed with three serious diseases all in one week back in May of 2010 – Lupus, Fibromyalgia, and Sjogren's. In February of 2012, she claimed she was diagnosed with Celiac Disease. By the time they got married at the end of the year in 2012, she claimed she was gluten intolerant too, and she insisted that her future mother-in-law and sister-in-law had cross-contaminated the food at one of the pre-wedding parties with non-gluten free foods so that she would not be able to eat.

To Christopher Watts, she said that she wanted to have ten children after he told her he wanted to have a big family. But to others, she claimed she was not able to have children because, she claimed, she had Endometriosis.

She would later claim that she needed fertility specialists in order to get pregnant – except she

MISS MENSA'S THEORY ~ on the Case of Christopher Watts Specific to Family Violence and Child Abuse is an opinion essay written to explore whether Christopher Watts is guilty of murdering his wife and their daughters beyond all reasonable doubt.

was pregnant with Bella within four months of the wedding and pregnant with Ce Ce when Bella was just ten months old.

One of their friends said that all she had to do was watch a commercial about a new illness, and she would claim to have that one too.

The day she was "missing", her friend told the police that she was diabetic.

Yet, according to Christopher Watts, moving to Colorado was a real-life saver because his wife was able to stop taking the 26 pills that she was taking daily when they lived in North Carolina.

When he spoke to the police, he said that his wife had Lupus, Rosacea, and that she took meds for her migraines.

That was it – no mention at all of diabetes, or Sjogren's, or Celiac, or Fibromyalgia, or Endometriosis, or any of the other diseases she claimed to have.

MISS MENSA'S THEORY ~ on the Case of Christopher Watts Specific to Family Violence and Child Abuse is an opinion essay written to explore whether Christopher Watts is guilty of murdering his wife and their daughters beyond all reasonable doubt.

And her autopsy stated that she was a healthy female.

I think she was a healthy female.

Physically healthy, that is.

And I think her BAC level listed on the autopsy report of .128 says it all. We're told that her BAC level was elevated due to decomposition. But I don't believe it. In one study, I learned that in studying over 275 bodies post-mortem with elevated BAC levels that only 20% of the levels were elevated due to non-alcohol related causes. And of those fifty-five or so which did register an elevated BAC that the average reading was half the BAC level of .128.

I think she was drunk the night she died. And I think drinking was a habit of hers, pregnant or not, based on her Facebook posts combined with that BAC level. However, if you listen to her friends, you'll hear them say that she would have never been drinking while pregnant, right? Yeah,

MISS MENSA'S THEORY ~ on the Case of Christopher Watts Specific to Family Violence and Child Abuse is an opinion essay written to explore whether Christopher Watts is guilty of murdering his wife and their daughters beyond all reasonable doubt.

okay. Those are the same friends who lined up her favorite "lemon drop" drinks in the middle of the table and sat there downing them as a "memorial" to her after she died.

Sorry, but if you're not a drinker then I highly doubt your friends are going to say let's all drink lemon drops in your honor.

I think she was a drinker and I think she liked her Oxy too. For her "migraines".

One point that I think is important to notice is that all the illnesses and diseases she claimed that she suffered from seem rather heavily dependent on patient reporting for any clinical diagnosis. Except for diabetes, which she never had, of course, in order to be diagnosed the doctor would rely heavily on whatever she was telling him. The same is true for the children's illnesses too. Asthma? Allergies? Stomach issues?

She claimed she had Lupus. She was in the sun whenever she wanted to be, and it was often.

MISS MENSA'S THEORY ~ on the Case of Christopher Watts Specific to Family Violence and Child Abuse is an opinion essay written to explore whether Christopher Watts is guilty of murdering his wife and their daughters beyond all reasonable doubt.

Fibromyalgia? Yet, she planned to work full-time and go to school full-time? Oh, wait. No, she didn't. It appears she just said that but when the time came for her to start that nursing program, she quit her job again. Oh, wait, that nursing program? Well, it appears she claims she made it through just one term.

I do not believe she was physically ill. At all. I think she was lying. And sadly, for Christopher Watts and for his family, and ultimately for his children, I think he was duped by her lies from day one.

I do believe she was ill, however. Just not physically ill, that's all. I believe that she suffered from either Bipolar, like her father-in-law mentioned in the interview, or from Schizophrenia, based on what appears to be two distinct personas presented in her social media activity and in her texting with her social media friends. I've been told by trusted sources that

MISS MENSA'S THEORY ~ on the Case of Christopher Watts Specific to Family Violence and Child Abuse is an opinion essay written to explore whether Christopher Watts is guilty of murdering his wife and their daughters beyond all reasonable doubt.

she had Bipolar. And maybe she did. But my hunch is that her mental illness was Schizophrenia. And I'll tell you why.

I think that "Shanann" was her personality who thought she was a nurse. The person making all those videos that she posted on social media before she died. The super excited, self-grandiose, all-knowing, all-powerful, super stay-at-home mom who was raking in the big bucks as a successful promoter for a multi-level marketing company.

And I think "Shannon" was her personality who was depressed, miserable, and afraid.

I think she had other personalities too – one being her "Veronica Horne" persona – the plain janes made pretty with their matching eyebrows.

The name "Veronica Horne" was one of her email addresses at the time of her death. I kid you not. Now wouldn't those emails be interesting to read.

MISS MENSA'S THEORY ~ on the Case of Christopher Watts Specific to Family Violence and Child Abuse is an opinion essay written to explore whether Christopher Watts is guilty of murdering his wife and their daughters beyond all reasonable doubt.

When she was younger, she supposedly suffered from migraines. I think she may have been suffering from something more. And I think that if you watch her videos closely that you just may agree.

Notice her limited vocabulary. Notice how at times she seems detached from those around her, especially her children.

Notice her difficulty in pronouncing simple words.

If she spends little time in that personality, then obviously she wouldn't have the opportunity to develop a well-rounded vocabulary. And it shows.

Her videos are all the same – Hey guys! Hey Dad! Hey Amanda, I mean Mandy, I mean Amanda. I'm so excited! Yummy. Look what just came in the mail! I'm so excited! Um. Um. Um. I've been up since four o'clock organizing my closets!

I could be wrong.

MISS MENSA'S THEORY ~ on the Case of Christopher Watts Specific to Family Violence and Child Abuse is an opinion essay written to explore whether Christopher Watts is guilty of murdering his wife and their daughters beyond all reasonable doubt.

It is possible that she was bipolar and that her "excited" personality in her videos were showing her manic phase while her "I can't do this" posts showing a depressed and miserable woman at the wheel could certainly represent her depressive phase.

And maybe my opinion is way off and she wasn't suffering from any mental illness or personality disorder at all. Maybe she was truly excited about promoting the MLMs she talked about in her videos.

Maybe her videos were all an act?

Or, maybe – she was truly caught up in the excitement that so many MLMs can bring to their followers' lives.

Even if only for a short time, until their promoters do the math and begin to realize the amount of money that they're spending compared to the actual amount they are bringing in. Maybe

MISS MENSA'S THEORY ~ on the Case of Christopher Watts Specific to Family Violence and Child Abuse is an opinion essay written to explore whether Christopher Watts is guilty of murdering his wife and their daughters beyond all reasonable doubt.

they finally realize they aren't really earning any money at all?

Her shopping sprees - regardless of the family's inability to pay - in my opinion - could be a sign of either mental illness mentioned, or her "excitement" over the MLMs she was promoting.

Fake it 'til you make it?

You must look and act successful before you'll ever be successful?

"Dress" the part?

According to the FTC statistics, you have a better chance at winning at the Roulette Wheel in Vegas than you do of ever seeing a dime of profit with a product-based multi-level marketing company.

In fact, the FTC reports that in the United States, 99.9% of people who are promoting a product based MLM will fail to ever see any profit at all.

MISS MENSA'S THEORY ~ on the Case of Christopher Watts Specific to Family Violence and Child Abuse is an opinion essay written to explore whether Christopher Watts is guilty of murdering his wife and their daughters beyond all reasonable doubt.

Yet, right from the start the same false narrative on the case that insisted she was a nurse who retired to become a stay-at-home mom, also insisted that she was a highly successful "employee" of an MLM and she was raking in 65k per year, she earned a free car, and she earned free trips too!

In fact, she was broke.

Flat broke.

The car she "earned" was a leased vehicle in her husband's name.

The trips? I highly doubt they were "free".

And I highly doubt she ever made any money at all with any of the MLMs she was promoting.

However, for what it's worth – I think that she honestly believed she was a huge success – depending on which personality, or mood, she was in.

MISS MENSA'S THEORY ~ on the Case of Christopher Watts Specific to Family Violence and Child Abuse is an opinion essay written to explore whether Christopher Watts is guilty of murdering his wife and their daughters beyond all reasonable doubt.

I am not bashing Christopher Watts' wife. At all. Nor have I ever.

I feel very sorry for her – because it seems that the same need for approval and attention and to be pretending that she was someone that she clearly was not – is quickly becoming her legacy on social media.

The attackers claim that she was and always will be a "saint".

While the people who are discussing the case on social media are learning more each day that shows she was far from it.

They claim she was intelligent, successful, beautiful, a great wife and mother who worked hard to support her family.

While the people who are discussing the case on social media are learning that maybe she wasn't intelligent, successful, or a great wife or mother at all.

MISS MENSA'S THEORY ~ on the Case of Christopher Watts Specific to Family Violence and Child Abuse is an opinion essay written to explore whether Christopher Watts is guilty of murdering his wife and their daughters beyond all reasonable doubt.

Whatever her videos show, the attackers have an answer – squirting poor little Bella in the face? They were just having a water fight. Except, Bella wasn't spraying anybody – she was standing there taking it – because when she ran to the slider and tried to get away from her mother spraying her right in the eyes, her mother said to her father – DON'T YOU SAVE HER. And he shut the door.

The attackers look at the WHACK-A-DADDY video – the one where Bella cries while her mother laughs – and say they were just having fun.

The attackers are not at all concerned about the photos showing the girls sleeping with blankets and pillows over their faces. The attackers are not at all concerned with the never-ending claims that the girls were both sick. The attackers say she was perfect. Because evidently, she isn't allowed to have been anything less.

MISS MENSA'S THEORY ~ on the Case of Christopher Watts Specific to Family Violence and Child Abuse is an opinion essay written to explore whether Christopher Watts is guilty of murdering his wife and their daughters beyond all reasonable doubt.

After watching her videos, reading her comments, and poring over the discovery documents too, I have concluded that it is quite possible that she didn't have any physical "health challenges" at all.

Some people discussing the case say they think she was a hypochondriac.

I don't agree.

Because a hypochondriac believes they have illnesses, right?

They worry. They wring their hands. They are afraid of dying.

Christopher Watts' wife seemed to enjoy mentioning her "health challenges" in such a way that she was some sort of superhero who could handle it all.

I think she had Munchausen. And I think when poor little Bella and Ce were born that she developed what is known as Munchausen by Proxy.

MISS MENSA'S THEORY ~ on the Case of Christopher Watts Specific to Family Violence and Child Abuse is an opinion essay written to explore whether Christopher Watts is guilty of murdering his wife and their daughters beyond all reasonable doubt.

I think she may have had schizophrenia – and that in her alter ego – that she was a nurse.

And tragically, for Bella and Ce Ce – I think she used the girls to fill in for the patients that in real-life the wannabe nurse would never have.

Think about the number of illnesses she claimed to have.

Think about the unlikelihood that ONE PERSON would have had all those illnesses and diseases.

Think about the fact that one family friend told the police that all she had to do was watch a commercial about an illness and she would say that she had that illness too.

Think.

Think about the fact that when her friend reported her missing that she told the police she had diabetes.

She NEVER had diabetes.

MISS MENSA'S THEORY ~ on the Case of Christopher Watts Specific to Family Violence and Child Abuse is an opinion essay written to explore whether Christopher Watts is guilty of murdering his wife and their daughters beyond all reasonable doubt.

THINK about how she claimed she was diagnosed with three serious diseases all within one week.

Think about how she claimed that at least on a monthly basis that the girls were sick.

Think about how when her friend stayed with her that the girls were healthy.

Think about how often she had other adults living right with her in her own home.

Think about how she said that she lost all her friends due to her "health challenges" but that was okay, according to her, because she made new friends online.

Think about the "heart butt challenge" – how she made a video and posted it right online showing her but in a pair of panties.

Think about how she used death language – dead, dying, kill, strangle, deathly, severely anaphylactic, deadly, she will strangle the dog, he will kill her for eating the MLM product that was

MISS MENSA'S THEORY ~ on the Case of Christopher Watts Specific to Family Violence and Child Abuse is an opinion essay written to explore whether Christopher Watts is guilty of murdering his wife and their daughters beyond all reasonable doubt.

just delivered before he gets home from work, etc.

And most alarming, of course, was when she had the nut meltdown at her in-laws' house and she yelled out that they didn't care if the girls lived or died.

She refused to allow her in-laws to ever see the girls after telling them that her daughters would never step foot in their house again.

She said that she would just "remove" them, presumably the grandparents, from their lives.

And one month later those poor babies were dead.

She's the same woman who asked her husband if he wanted her to get an abortion. She's the same woman who asked her husband if he would stay with her if they didn't have kids.

She's the same woman who convinced her husband that she was taking 26 pills per day for all her

MISS MENSA'S THEORY ~ on the Case of Christopher Watts Specific to Family Violence and Child Abuse is an opinion essay written to explore whether Christopher Watts is guilty of murdering his wife and their daughters beyond all reasonable doubt.

serious diseases – then convinced him that simply by moving to Colorado that she was able to stop taking 26 pills per day. She said that the "weather" in Colorado helped 95% of her diseases.

Look at the statistics – the chances of a woman at her age having all the diseases she claimed to have are nil.

The same is true for her claims about the girls – the chances of two little girls both suffering so many illnesses and conditions and diseases and needing certain procedures and having so many allergies and breathing problems and, and, and, don't forget FAMILIAL MEDITERRANEAN FEVER – well, the chances that her claims were true?

Zero.

MISS MENSA'S THEORY ~ on the Case of Christopher Watts Specific to Family Violence and Child Abuse is an opinion essay written to explore whether Christopher Watts is guilty of murdering his wife and their daughters beyond all reasonable doubt.

Doctor's Orders?

Christopher Watts' wife convinced him before they were even married that her doctor told her she had to move to Colorado for her "health challenges". Have you ever heard of such a thing as a doctor telling a patient they had to move to Colorado? I think that she may have had an appointment with a doctor shortly before she told Christopher Watts that she had to move. But my hunch is that the doctor's appointment went something like this – instead of any doctor telling her to move – I think a doctor may well have said – I want you to see a psychiatrist. You do not have any of the diseases you claim to have. You are physically healthy. But I am referring you to the psychiatrist for a full psych-eval so we can

MISS MENSA'S THEORY ~ on the Case of Christopher Watts Specific to Family Violence and Child Abuse is an opinion essay written to explore whether Christopher Watts is guilty of murdering his wife and their daughters beyond all reasonable doubt.

get to the bottom of your need to believe that you have serious physical health problems.

She said that back when she was first diagnosed with her "health challenges" that she lost her friends because they just didn't understand what she was going through. I think if she did have any friends and she lost them it was more likely they figured out exactly what she was going through – and they told her to get help. She said that when she lost all her friends that she made new friends online. Think about it – if you're a con, or delusional, then it would be much easier to maintain friendships online than in real life. And it appears that trying to have friends on social media was exactly how she was able to continue to claim that she suffered from so many diseases, which I highly suspect were all lies.

The same is true for that nursing program that she claimed she was magically accepted into. In one of her online discussions with a "friend", at

MISS MENSA'S THEORY ~ on the Case of Christopher Watts Specific to Family Violence and Child Abuse is an opinion essay written to explore whether Christopher Watts is guilty of murdering his wife and their daughters beyond all reasonable doubt.

first, I thought that the two women knew each other. But evidently, they didn't because at the end of their conversation she asked her "friend" what she was going to school for.

Even one of her cousins was kept at a distance on social media it seems when she said to her – what state do you live in? Did Christopher Watts' wife have any friends of her own? The one who reported her missing didn't know how old she was. Some of the friends interviewed by the police had met her just once or twice. And it seemed all of them were from the same MLMs that she belonged to so maybe they were "friends" through their mutual efforts to "build their MLM teams". But did she have a friend, a real-life friend, who could have looked her in the eyes and said Honey, there's something wrong and we need to get you some help? Could that be exactly what a doctor said to her when she suddenly told Christopher Watts that she had to move to Colorado?

MISS MENSA'S THEORY ~ on the Case of Christopher Watts Specific to Family Violence and Child Abuse is an opinion essay written to explore whether Christopher Watts is guilty of murdering his wife and their daughters beyond all reasonable doubt.

Isolation from Family and Friends

In an interview given by Christopher Watts' parents, his father said that he believed his daughter-in-law was bipolar. I agree that she was either bipolar or schizophrenic. In the same interview, the grieving grandparents also said they believed their daughter-in-law was attempting to isolate their son from his family. And I think they were right.

I think she was trying to isolate Christopher Watts from his family members and from his life-long friends from the day the two of them went on their first date, in fact. One of his friends told me that she was rude to them from the time he first started to include her in their get-togethers. She would outright insult his friends

---

MISS MENSA'S THEORY ~ on the Case of Christopher Watts Specific to Family Violence and Child Abuse is an opinion essay written to explore whether Christopher Watts is guilty of murdering his wife and their daughters beyond all reasonable doubt.

and then later he would sheepishly apologize for her rudeness and say that she was just having a bad day.

She told him he could no longer go to the gym daily, or at all, because she didn't want him to be working out with any of his ex-girlfriends. She became irate when he hugged the wife of one of his close friends, and they didn't see that couple again for a very long time. I think the move to Colorado served a couple of purposes for her – because I think her doctor wanted her to see a psychiatrist and she decided to get out of town fast instead. And I also think that by moving far away from his family and friends that it was easier for her to pull the wool right over his eyes.

He had a high-paying job, a good savings account, and excellent credit when he met her. He owned his dream Mustang too. He was fit and enjoyed working out at the gym every day. And he was surrounded by loving family members and life-long

MISS MENSA'S THEORY ~ on the Case of Christopher Watts Specific to Family Violence and Child Abuse is an opinion essay written to explore whether Christopher Watts is guilty of murdering his wife and their daughters beyond all reasonable doubt.

friends. In Colorado, he took a lower paying job, his savings was depleted, his credit was about to be shot as soon as he married her, his Mustang was history, and he was no longer fit since she didn't like him working out at the gym.

And his loving family members and life-long friends were now 1,600 miles away.

Evidently, the physical distance wasn't quite good enough for his wife – since it seems she was trying to break the bond between him and his family for good. She accused her future mother-in-law and sister-in-law of cross contaminating the food at one of the pre-wedding parties. She fired his sister from the bridal party when she told her to take the entire week of the wedding off work and his sister told her that was not possible.

She told him that his mother was rude to her at one of the pre-wedding parties and had him call his mother on the phone and tell her that she

---

MISS MENSA'S THEORY ~ on the Case of Christopher Watts Specific to Family Violence and Child Abuse is an opinion essay written to explore whether Christopher Watts is guilty of murdering his wife and their daughters beyond all reasonable doubt.

embarrassed him by being rude to his future wife – three days before the big day.

When his family did not attend the wedding in late 2012, in my opinion, his bride had achieved her goal.

Fast forward to 2018 shortly before her death. Their marriage was on the rocks. She told a hair stylist in July of 2018 that she was getting a divorce. Before that, back in late March, she peppered a stranger in a restaurant who she learned was a lawyer with all sorts of questions about divorce and custody.

I think she had to go to North Carolina for six weeks in the summer because based on what I've been told by reliable sources, and because I think it's reasonable to believe what I've been told, I do not believe she was allowed to be alone with Bella and Ce Ce. And I don't think they had the money to pay for the summer program at the daycare center.

MISS MENSA'S THEORY ~ on the Case of Christopher Watts Specific to Family Violence and Child Abuse is an opinion essay written to explore whether Christopher Watts is guilty of murdering his wife and their daughters beyond all reasonable doubt.

So, there she was in North Carolina for six weeks, and as she put it, stuck with the kids while her husband was living the life of a bachelor, so it seems rather obvious that being alone with her own children was not exactly her forte'.

At one point while staying at her in-laws' house, when her mother-in-law left in the morning to go get her hair done, she called suddenly out of the blue and told her that she had to return home immediately. She said WHO IS GOING TO TAKE CARE OF THE KIDS and YOU CAN'T LEAVE ME HERE WITH THE KIDS!

Her mother-in-law thought to herself WHOA, THEY'RE YOUR KIDS as she sat there staring at her cell phone wondering what on earth her daughter-in-law's problem was with being alone with her own children for an hour or two.

This adds credibility to the claims people who have contacted me have made - they say that she was caught medically abusing the both girls in

MISS MENSA'S THEORY ~ on the Case of Christopher Watts Specific to Family Violence and Child Abuse is an opinion essay written to explore whether Christopher Watts is guilty of murdering his wife and their daughters beyond all reasonable doubt.

December of 2016. Then after fourteen months of not being allowed any time alone with the girls, the "family plan" was expanded to allow her to spend 90 minutes per day alone with the girls in order to get them off to daycare in the mornings after her husband left for work.

So, it makes sense that after an hour with her mother-in-law off getting her hair done that she was freaking out if she knew that it was against the "family plan" for her to be alone with the girls more than 90 minutes per day.

The nut meltdown at her in-laws' house was yet another opportunity for her in-laws to see a side to her they feared had existed all along.

The official narrative reads that she was upset because her in-laws gave the girls nuts, even though they were "severely anaphylactic" and "deathly allergic" to nuts, though there is some confusion on whether it's supposedly tree nuts or peanuts the girls were "allergic" to.

MISS MENSA'S THEORY ~ on the Case of Christopher Watts Specific to Family Violence and Child Abuse is an opinion essay written to explore whether Christopher Watts is guilty of murdering his wife and their daughters beyond all reasonable doubt.

We've heard it all – that Papa gave the girls ice cream with nuts on top, that Papa ate ice cream near them with nuts on top, that Auntie placed a bowl of nuts right on the counter, that it was really a bowl of chocolate kisses that sent her flying over the edge, that it was ice cream given to the girls that was manufactured in a plant that also processes tree nuts, that it was actually a bag of pistachios on the shelf...

You name it and those evil grandparents did it, to be sure, according to the narrative. Also, according to their daughter-in-law, they had RAZOR BLADES LAYING ALL OVER THE HOUSE!

In my opinion, the girls were not allergic to anything at all. And in my opinion, her conniption fit supposedly over nut allergies because I think she was her final effort to set the stage for her husband and her children to never see her in-laws again.

MISS MENSA'S THEORY ~ on the Case of Christopher Watts Specific to Family Violence and Child Abuse is an opinion essay written to explore whether Christopher Watts is guilty of murdering his wife and their daughters beyond all reasonable doubt.

I do not believe his parents ever put either child at risk of being exposed to any nut. Like I said, I highly doubt the girls had any allergies at all. And even if they did, I highly doubt that Christopher Watts' mother or father or sister would have ever placed either child in harm's way.

I think that Christopher Watts' wife suffered some sort of a breakdown while she was visiting her in-laws. She went from acting normal to having an evil black look in her eyes. She started screaming. She hollered about the razor blades laying all over the house that evidently existed only in her own mind. And she yelled that her in-laws didn't care whether the children lived or died.

When I was a police dispatcher with the State Police, had a call like this come in, I would have sent, lights and sirens, emergency medical help for her to be taken in for evaluation. But they didn't dial 911. They ran out the door with the

MISS MENSA'S THEORY ~ on the Case of Christopher Watts Specific to Family Violence and Child Abuse is an opinion essay written to explore whether Christopher Watts is guilty of murdering his wife and their daughters beyond all reasonable doubt.

children and drove around for a while wringing their hands and trying to calm their grandchildren down after the frightening sight that they had all just suffered from having to see. After a while they returned to the house hoping she had calmed down by then – but she hadn't. She was shaking. She was furious. And she told them that HER DAUGHTERS WOULD NEVER STEP FOOT IN THEIR HOUSE AGAIN.

She was right, of course, because poor little Bella and Ce Ce never got to see their beloved Mimi and Papa again - since the girls were both smothered to death just one month after the major nut meltdown occurred.

Now, think about this. Remember that wedding? Remember how just three days before the wedding she expected her soon to be husband to call his mother and tell her she was rude and embarrassing? Remember how she had fired her sister-in-law from the bridal party when she said

MISS MENSA'S THEORY ~ on the Case of Christopher Watts Specific to Family Violence and Child Abuse is an opinion essay written to explore whether Christopher Watts is guilty of murdering his wife and their daughters beyond all reasonable doubt.

that she was not able to take the entire week off work leading up to the wedding day? Remember how she accused his mom and sister of "cross-contaminating" the food so that the poor gluten intolerant femme fatale would not be able to eat?

Well, I think her GOAL was to make damn sure his family DID NOT attend the wedding. And of course, her tactics worked because they did not feel at all welcome, or safe, to attend their own son's wedding.

Now, compare that to the nut meltdown six years later. Was history repeating itself? Big wedding – so offend, fight, cry, whine, and make damn sure they don't feel welcome to attend. Ce Ce's birthday party was set to take place shortly after the nut meltdown. It was going to be a huge family affair. A big party. A huge group of people. Hmm. Could it be that she staged her ridiculous nut meltdown because she wanted to make damn

---

MISS MENSA'S THEORY ~ on the Case of Christopher Watts Specific to Family Violence and Child Abuse is an opinion essay written to explore whether Christopher Watts is guilty of murdering his wife and their daughters beyond all reasonable doubt.

sure that his family would not feel welcome, or feel that it was safe, to attend?

Bella and Ce Ce's beloved "Mimi" and "Papa" did not attend the birthday party. And I don't blame them one bit. Just imagine the garbage that came out of their daughter-in-law's mouth. Would you have attended the birthday party after your daughter-in-law screamed at you that you didn't care if your grandchildren lived or died? She also gave her mother-in-law a big F.U. on social media following her meltdown at her in-laws' house. Seriously, would you attend the birthday party right after she accused them of trying to harm their grandchildren?

For six years straight she used the fact his parents didn't go to the wedding to play the victim. And when they didn't go to the birthday party she did it again. Boo hoo. Your parents are so mean. Boo hoo. They don't care about our

---

MISS MENSA'S THEORY ~ on the Case of Christopher Watts Specific to Family Violence and Child Abuse is an opinion essay written to explore whether Christopher Watts is guilty of murdering his wife and their daughters beyond all reasonable doubt.

children. Boo hoo. You better never speak to them again.

When he flew to North Carolina for the final week of the "vacation" and went to visit his parents, she refused to "allow" him to take the girls with him to their house.

Then after he was there visiting his mom and dad for just a short while, she called him and told him that it was time for him to return to her parents' house where she was with their daughters. He told her that he was going to spend the night at his parents' house.

And she said OH, NO YOU'RE NOT!

He said that he was – and that he would see her the next day. And she said that she was on her way to pick him up. He folded. Instead of standing up for himself – he asked his dad to give him a ride back to her parents' house.

MISS MENSA'S THEORY ~ on the Case of Christopher Watts Specific to Family Violence and Child Abuse is an opinion essay written to explore whether Christopher Watts is guilty of murdering his wife and their daughters beyond all reasonable doubt.

When they sent a present for Ce Ce, she had her friend grab it fast after it was delivered and send it right on back.

When they went to Myrtle Beach and Mimi and Papa were also in Myrtle Beach and staying just five miles away, she REFUSED TO ALLOW them to see their granddaughters.

Obviously, she expected her husband to cut all ties at that point with his family.

But he refused. Instead, he saw through her games, her antics, her bad acts.

And he told her they were through.

The irony in all of this is that while she was lying about his parents and ridiculing them to boot in what appears to have been her final attempt to isolate him completely from his family, she was actually saying to her friends that she was trying to save her marriage. Yeah, okay.

MISS MENSA'S THEORY ~ on the Case of Christopher Watts Specific to Family Violence and Child Abuse is an opinion essay written to explore whether Christopher Watts is guilty of murdering his wife and their daughters beyond all reasonable doubt.

Saving her marriage? Or was it all really her last-ditch effort to regain total power and control over her husband by "removing" any contact at all that he and their children had with his family?

In one of her more wicked posts online she said that she would just "remove" them as if cutting all ties with her husband's family members was a perfectly fine choice for his wife to make. Or, could it be that it wasn't his parents she was talking about?

Remember that shortly before Bella and Ce Ce were murdered, their mother asked their dad if he would stay with her if they didn't have kids. She also asked her husband if he thought she should get an abortion.

MISS MENSA'S THEORY ~ on the Case of Christopher Watts Specific to Family Violence and Child Abuse is an opinion essay written to explore whether Christopher Watts is guilty of murdering his wife and their daughters beyond all reasonable doubt.

Was Christopher Watts a Battered Husband?

In my opinion, Christopher Watts was a battered husband. I do not believe he committed the crimes that he pleaded guilty to. However, I do believe he feels responsible for the tragedy. I do believe he blames himself.

Because that's what battered spouses do.

Battered spouses are groomed to believe that no matter what goes wrong, it's their fault. Battered spouses are conditioned to stay. Battered spouses are convinced, at a very deep level, that if only they weren't so weak, or so stupid, or so careless, or so lazy, ugly, fat, fill in the blank – then their abuser would not have done what they did.

In some cases of spousal abuse, it can take many years after the abusive relationship ends for the

---

MISS MENSA'S THEORY ~ on the Case of Christopher Watts Specific to Family Violence and Child Abuse is an opinion essay written to explore whether Christopher Watts is guilty of murdering his wife and their daughters beyond all reasonable doubt.

battered spouse to recognize that what their abusers did was not their fault.

Survivors of spousal abuse blame themselves for the failure of the marriage, for the abuse they endured, and for the way their abuser treated them, sometimes forever, and sometimes for a very long time after they are no longer being abused. Because battered spouses not only blame themselves for whatever the abuser has done, they are conditioned from the start, groomed, taught, brainwashed to believe that it's all their fault and also their job to always cover for their abuser's bad acts.

When his wife had the nut meltdown in 2018, her in-laws were exposed to seeing her darkness, her anger, her temper, her rage. And it frightened them, and the children too, of course.

Well, according to Christopher Watts, he lived with her anger and resentment toward his family for six years straight.

MISS MENSA'S THEORY ~ on the Case of Christopher Watts Specific to Family Violence and Child Abuse is an opinion essay written to explore whether Christopher Watts is guilty of murdering his wife and their daughters beyond all reasonable doubt.

Primarily, she would verbally abuse him. But one time, he saw her physically act out her anger and resentment – and it wasn't pretty folks.

It was the one time that he stood up to her in their marriage. And it didn't go so well.

For him, anyway. For her, it was all it took for him to learn that it was not safe to ever speak up to her again.

She was so angry with him for talking back, that she immediately kicked him right out of the house.

And by the time he could return, the lesson was learned, and he never again spoke up to his wife.

Sell his car? Sure! Buy a house they couldn't afford? Of course! Buy furniture and clothes and trips they couldn't pay for? Why not?

If she wanted it, she got it. No questions asked. Because he learned early on in their marriage

---

MISS MENSA'S THEORY ~ on the Case of Christopher Watts Specific to Family Violence and Child Abuse is an opinion essay written to explore whether Christopher Watts is guilty of murdering his wife and their daughters beyond all reasonable doubt.

that it was safer to simply say YES DEAR or SURE HONEY or OH, OKAY.

He had already suffered through seeing her rage filled tantrum - and he did not want to ever have to go through that again. He says it happened just once in their marriage, very early on, out of the blue.

Remember that he said he had made the "mistake" of speaking up.

And she blew a gasket.

She attacked him.

She raged.

He watched as her temper exploded.

And it frightened him.

And within just minutes, he was forced out of their home.

I think that's the day that Christopher Watts learned to never speak up again.

MISS MENSA'S THEORY ~ on the Case of Christopher Watts Specific to Family Violence and Child Abuse is an opinion essay written to explore whether Christopher Watts is guilty of murdering his wife and their daughters beyond all reasonable doubt.

That's the day that he learned there was nothing at all worth ever tapping into his wife's deeply buried rage again.

That's the day, in my opinion, that Christopher Watts became a battered spouse.

When I speak on the issues of domestic violence and child abuse, I'm contacted by the attendees who want to tell me their stories of the abuses they have suffered through. And repeatedly, their stories are the same as they remember the ONE TIME their spouse exploded. Or the ONE TIME they were hit.

Abusers know it only takes one time to gain control. And the day that Christopher Watts spoke up, and was blasted by his wife's high-powered rage against him, was all it took for him to learn to NEVER speak up again – to NEVER question her again – to NEVER hold her responsible for her own actions – because it clearly wasn't safe for him to speak.

MISS MENSA'S THEORY ~ on the Case of Christopher Watts Specific to Family Violence and Child Abuse is an opinion essay written to explore whether Christopher Watts is guilty of murdering his wife and their daughters beyond all reasonable doubt.

In fact, I think that from the first day they met that Christopher Watts was covering for his wife's bad acts – even before she exploded and kicked him out of the house for talking back to her.

Because from day one of their relationship I think he truly believed all her lies. I think he truly believed that she was superhuman. I think he truly believed that she was smarter than he was, and stronger than he was, and downright "better" than he was.

So, by the time she exploded and kicked him out of the house clearly showing him who the boss was in that relationship – I think it already established from day one that she was perfect and if he doubted it then all he had to do was ask her for clarification.

By the time she had her full blown temper tantrum and kicked him out of the house – I think by then he was already groomed to believe that

MISS MENSA'S THEORY ~ on the Case of Christopher Watts Specific to Family Violence and Child Abuse is an opinion essay written to explore whether Christopher Watts is guilty of murdering his wife and their daughters beyond all reasonable doubt.

any of her bad behavior, any of their financial problems, any of her "flares" she claimed to have from her many "health challenges", any of her struggles were ALL HIS FAULT.

I think she was highly skilled at claiming the credit, no pun intended, for all the good and dumping the blame for anything negative onto him.

That's what abusers do.

Which is why it takes many survivors of abuse a very long time to begin to see their abuser for who they really are. They internalize the blame. For everything.

The question looms, of course, if he didn't murder his daughters, as he claimed he didn't in that police interview, then why would he have accepted the plea deal that required him to plead guilty to murdering them.

MISS MENSA'S THEORY ~ on the Case of Christopher Watts Specific to Family Violence and Child Abuse is an opinion essay written to explore whether Christopher Watts is guilty of murdering his wife and their daughters beyond all reasonable doubt.

Well, if my opinion is "right" then it makes sense. Because if he was taking the blame for everything right from the start, while simultaneously believing that his wife was all-powerful, all-knowing, a real super star, etc. then it seems obvious he would use the same thought processes when analyzing what happened to the girls.

He was having an affair that summer while his wife and kids were in North Carolina.

He was standing up to his wife.

He was talking back.

He was seeing through her anger and rage and recognizing that the way she was treating his family was her problem, not theirs.

He told her he wanted a divorce.

So, if he was telling the truth when he said that she murdered their daughters, then it makes perfect sense he would blame himself for her actions.

MISS MENSA'S THEORY ~ on the Case of Christopher Watts Specific to Family Violence and Child Abuse is an opinion essay written to explore whether Christopher Watts is guilty of murdering his wife and their daughters beyond all reasonable doubt.

There's another point to consider along these same lines – Christopher Watts grew up attending church every Sunday morning. He was taught all about heaven and hell.

And he was taught all about the husband's role in the marriage – being the spiritual leader of the family.

He was taught that murdering someone meant that you go to hell.

Yes, he was taught about forgiveness. But the teachings about murder and hell are very powerful, especially for children, to hear from the pulpit all his life.

If it's true what he said that his wife murdered their daughters then he will absolutely be feeling a strong spiritual need to believe that his wife IS NOT in hell. Maybe his need to believe it is so strong that he chooses instead to keep lying? Maybe the need to believe it is so strong that he is continuing to lie to himself? Either way, it is all

MISS MENSA'S THEORY ~ on the Case of Christopher Watts Specific to Family Violence and Child Abuse is an opinion essay written to explore whether Christopher Watts is guilty of murdering his wife and their daughters beyond all reasonable doubt.

his fault, the tragedy, no matter which way he looks at it. Whether he killed his daughters or his wife did, as he claimed, he will harbor the guilt and the blame for either or both of their actions probably for many years to come.

Obviously, if he killed his children then he will continue to say that he did it. And I think it's also obvious that if he was telling the truth when he said that she killed their daughters that he will continue to blame himself for her actions until the day he dies.

MISS MENSA'S THEORY ~ on the Case of Christopher Watts Specific to Family Violence and Child Abuse is an opinion essay written to explore whether Christopher Watts is guilty of murdering his wife and their daughters beyond all reasonable doubt.

Blurred Boundaries

In abusive relationships there are blurred boundaries which serve to allow the abusive partner to gain and to maintain total power and control over their victim spouse. In later years, she tells the story of when she first knew that he was her man – she says that she was laying across his lap sleeping and that she laid there for hours and he never said a word.

He had to use the bathroom.

But he didn't ask her to move so he could get up and use the bathroom.

He sat there.

Waiting.

She thought that was a cute story to tell? How he sat there for hours silently waiting for her to move so he could use the john? But to those of us

---

MISS MENSA'S THEORY ~ on the Case of Christopher Watts Specific to Family Violence and Child Abuse is an opinion essay written to explore whether Christopher Watts is guilty of murdering his wife and their daughters beyond all reasonable doubt.

who have researched domestic violence extensively, that story really isn't very cute at all.

It's an illustration of how she violated his boundaries – which abusers are known to do. She didn't care about his needs, and he learned not to care about his own needs either.

This kind of reminds me of the attackers online – they don't care at all about the people they are abusing – or recognize how their actions are trampling on our rights. Because to abusers, their victims are not people. They are objects instead. Objects to use, to insult, to batter, while the abusers themselves pretend they are special, or smart, or the one person who "deserves" to be treated well.

Another way that boundaries are violated early on in an abusive marriage, which I think occurred in the case of Christopher Watts, is when the abuser tells a series of lies without caring at all about their partner's ability to trust them.

MISS MENSA'S THEORY ~ on the Case of Christopher Watts Specific to Family Violence and Child Abuse is an opinion essay written to explore whether Christopher Watts is guilty of murdering his wife and their daughters beyond all reasonable doubt.

Abusers are liars – again, just look at the attackers online who have been attacking us for thirteen months straight – they wouldn't know the truth if it smacked them upside the head – they lie their way through without ever giving it a thought how easy it is for people to see what they're really made of.

But in an intimate relationship, it isn't quite so easy to see. She learned what mattered to him, then she proceeded to lie in order to basically give him what he wanted – what he needed to hear – for her to latch onto him, and his income stream – for life.

He wanted a big family, so she said she wanted ten kids. He went to trade school so she said she wanted to further her education. His sister was a medical professional, so she said she wanted to become a nurse.

And he believed her.

And he also believed it was possible.

MISS MENSA'S THEORY ~ on the Case of Christopher Watts Specific to Family Violence and Child Abuse is an opinion essay written to explore whether Christopher Watts is guilty of murdering his wife and their daughters beyond all reasonable doubt.

Liars keep their victims busy with all the drama they create – remember the break in while she claimed she was in the house. Remember the 26 pills she claimed she had to take each day and how she claimed the weather in Colorado magically helped her with 95% of her diseases.

Remember the list of diseases. Remember how she posted about her constant "flares".

And remember how she lied about his family and friends right from the start of the relationship. They were rude to her. They were SOOO rude to her that she demanded he call them to tell them that they were rude to her. And he did.

That's domestic violence 101.

She was nice, she was hard-working, she was so smart, she was so brave to overcome so many major illnesses and disease.

Except she wasn't.

She was a fake.

MISS MENSA'S THEORY ~ on the Case of Christopher Watts Specific to Family Violence and Child Abuse is an opinion essay written to explore whether Christopher Watts is guilty of murdering his wife and their daughters beyond all reasonable doubt.

She was a liar.

And she was swooping in to snatch him up in her self-created web of lies.

Here is the truth - for six years straight, between the wedding and the nut meltdown, she got along just fine with her in-laws. To their face anyway. Because behind closed doors she made his life a living hell by CONSTANTLY berating his parents.

It was the topic that she used daily to abuse her husband with.

Your mother is psycho.

Your mother is mean.

Your mother is stupid.

Your sister is a whore.

Your sister is a bitch.

Your sister is a loser.

Your mother and sister are both rude to me.

MISS MENSA'S THEORY ~ on the Case of Christopher Watts Specific to Family Violence and Child Abuse is an opinion essay written to explore whether Christopher Watts is guilty of murdering his wife and their daughters beyond all reasonable doubt.

Your father is just like you, a dummy.

Your father is a wimp.

To their faces, she showed her superficial side. The fake smiles. The fake compliments. The fake stories. And behind their backs, they were the scum of the earth.

For six years straight.

She hated them. And she expected her husband to hate them too.

Just imagine the emotional and physical fatigue he must have felt during the entire time he was with her.

The daily attacks against his own family members that never seemed to end while at the same time she was claiming that she and her first mother-in-law were close.

I doubt it.

I'll just betcha her first mother-in-law has been celebrating her son's divorce for years.

MISS MENSA'S THEORY ~ on the Case of Christopher Watts Specific to Family Violence and Child Abuse is an opinion essay written to explore whether Christopher Watts is guilty of murdering his wife and their daughters beyond all reasonable doubt.

Yet, Christopher Watts' wife claimed her first mother-in-loved her. She claimed her first mother-in-law NEVER had a problem with her.

Dig in deeper to that little storyline – do you believe that her first mother-in-law never had a problem with her? Do you believe they were close?

I don't.

But imagine how that storyline was weaved into the abuse – something like this – "Well, I don't know what YOUR mother's problem is, my first mother-in-law loves me!" or "Your mother obviously is the one with a problem because my first mother-in-law and I are close so surely it isn't because of me that your mother is acting so strange".

Keep in mind that to their faces, she acted like everything was just fine. But to her husband, she acted as if his family members were worthless pieces of shit.

MISS MENSA'S THEORY ~ on the Case of Christopher Watts Specific to Family Violence and Child Abuse is an opinion essay written to explore whether Christopher Watts is guilty of murdering his wife and their daughters beyond all reasonable doubt.

His family members.

The people he loved.

The people that she was evidently afraid just might one day be able to talk some sense into him and he would be able to see that his wife was abusing him.

In my opinion, from day one she did her best to isolate him from his family members and his life-long friends.

Again, that's what abusers do.

Because they do not want someone to care enough to take their victim aside and say HEY, YOU DESERVE BETTER THAN TO BE TREATED LIKE SHE'S TREATING YOU.

MISS MENSA'S THEORY ~ on the Case of Christopher Watts Specific to Family Violence and Child Abuse is an opinion essay written to explore whether Christopher Watts is guilty of murdering his wife and their daughters beyond all reasonable doubt.

Identity Erosion

Once the abuser is able to isolate his or her victim spouse from their family members and friends, as Christopher Watts' wife appears to have succeeded in doing as soon as she convinced

MISS MENSA'S THEORY ~ on the Case of Christopher Watts Specific to Family Violence and Child Abuse is an opinion essay written to explore whether Christopher Watts is guilty of murdering his wife and their daughters beyond all reasonable doubt.

him to move to Colorado, and then even more when she conned him into calling his folks to tell them they were "rude" right before the wedding – the next step was to blur the boundaries between her and her husband – so that her husband would learn to stop thinking for himself.

Once the boundaries were blurred – she was then able to begin to erode his identity, as if having a separate identity was not allowed.

In domestic violence cases, victims are led to believe that having an identity separate from the abuser's is selfish, and wrong.

Look at how she conned him into believing that he should not continue to go to the gym daily, or even at all, if he wanted to be in a relationship with her.

She did not want him working out at the gym? That's right, folks. Because she did not want to risk having him run into one of his ex-girlfriends. That is a prime example of an abuser expecting to

MISS MENSA'S THEORY ~ on the Case of Christopher Watts Specific to Family Violence and Child Abuse is an opinion essay written to explore whether Christopher Watts is guilty of murdering his wife and their daughters beyond all reasonable doubt.

have total power and control over their victim. It is also a prime example of a person, the abuser, who is insecure. He enjoyed working out daily at the gym. It's part of who he was. Remember that he was an athlete in high school. He enjoyed actively taking part in sports, as a team member, competing together against the other teams, and giving it his best.

He enjoyed working out at the gym the same way that he enjoyed taking part in sports while he was in school – the comradery, the encouragement from others, being part of the "team".

The attackers say that he was some sort of a social outcast or that he was awkward in any social setting. NOT TRUE. The attackers say that she was the social butterfly while he was the dork with no friends. But the attackers, as usual, have it backwards. Because he was the one who was comfortable in a social setting, including going to the gym. And it was his wife who seemed

---

MISS MENSA'S THEORY ~ on the Case of Christopher Watts Specific to Family Violence and Child Abuse is an opinion essay written to explore whether Christopher Watts is guilty of murdering his wife and their daughters beyond all reasonable doubt.

incapable of making healthy social connections for the entirety of their relationship based on the way she treated his friends and family members right from the start.

Who was Christopher Watts when he met her? He was successful. He had life-long friends. He came from a family that loved him, that was stable, and that did not engage in any drama at all.

Christopher Watts came from a good home, a good family, a solid, well-rounded, healthy family with strong ties to each other and bonded by love.

Not by anger. Not by drama. Not by fear.

His family is honest, hard-working, and kind. So, when he met his future wife, that was the only template that he had ever known, and he expected that other people followed that same template too. He was trusting. He was gullible. He was naïve.

MISS MENSA'S THEORY ~ on the Case of Christopher Watts Specific to Family Violence and Child Abuse is an opinion essay written to explore whether Christopher Watts is guilty of murdering his wife and their daughters beyond all reasonable doubt.

And he felt safe. Because he was safe.

Before he met her, that is.

I think in the case of Christopher Watts that he came from a place of true confidence and a sense of safety, stability, and love.

And I think his wife wanted to be a part of his family, a member of the Watts' tribe, but I think she had issues that prevented her from ever feeling like she truly belonged. I think that she felt "less than" – a term she would use six years later specific to her children – that she never wanted them to feel "less than" when she was talking about the evil and dangerous world that we live in.

I think that she was very insecure, and that she was trying hard to fit in but that maybe she just didn't know how to fit in with his family members or with his life-long friends either. So, I think she put on a superficial smile then proceeded to

MISS MENSA'S THEORY ~ on the Case of Christopher Watts Specific to Family Violence and Child Abuse is an opinion essay written to explore whether Christopher Watts is guilty of murdering his wife and their daughters beyond all reasonable doubt.

try to convince them, and herself, that she was some sort of superpower-chick.

As if maybe she didn't realize right from the start that his family loved her and accepted her for who she was, not for whoever she may have been pretending to be.

Christopher Watts' family was one that led a simple life – they vacationed each summer – to visit their relatives. They weren't into fancy cars, or houses, or clothes. They were into family dinners and hugs and taking care of grandma. They were into taking care of their kids and welcoming their kids' friends into their home. They were into supporting their children's goals and dreams and helping to make it possible for their children to succeed.

I think that his wife saw his family and felt threatened by their authenticity, their genuine love for each other, their automatic acceptance of her too, not because she was some sort of

MISS MENSA'S THEORY ~ on the Case of Christopher Watts Specific to Family Violence and Child Abuse is an opinion essay written to explore whether Christopher Watts is guilty of murdering his wife and their daughters beyond all reasonable doubt.

superstar or huge success, as she appeared to have claimed to be, but they loved her simply because their son loved her, that's what families do.

But back to the jealousy thing – I think that she was used to being the center of attention when she met him – or that she strived to be the center of attention anyway – and I think when she met his sister that she saw her as a challenge – as her nemesis – as someone who actually had what it was that she wanted for herself but maybe didn't know how to set goals and work hard to reach her goals like his sister obviously knew how to do.

I think she saw her beauty, and her career, and her close ties with her family and sadly I think she felt "less than".

But she wasn't "less than" and I don't believe for one second that his family ever said or did anything that would make her feel "less than" at all.

MISS MENSA'S THEORY ~ on the Case of Christopher Watts Specific to Family Violence and Child Abuse is an opinion essay written to explore whether Christopher Watts is guilty of murdering his wife and their daughters beyond all reasonable doubt.

I think she missed an opportunity early on to just be happy, content, safe, and secure. Because instead, I think she set out to be "more than" his sister was, and that's not how self-confidence and personal achievement works.

Remember the wedding? Remember the nut meltdown?

She fired his sister from the wedding party. Right? That's huge, you guys. That is huge.

Six years later, her nut meltdown happened within minutes of his sister showing up at her in-laws' house.

She was fine. Everybody was getting along just fine. Her mother-in-law had taken her to the grocery store when she first arrived, and she paid $325 for her to be able to choose whatever she wanted to have in the house for her and the girls. She had a long list of allergies that she claimed the girls had plus she claimed she was gluten intolerant and that she had celiac too,

MISS MENSA'S THEORY ~ on the Case of Christopher Watts Specific to Family Violence and Child Abuse is an opinion essay written to explore whether Christopher Watts is guilty of murdering his wife and their daughters beyond all reasonable doubt.

right? So, her mother-in-law wanted her to have exactly whatever foods she wanted.

The Watts family is not wealthy at all. They're hard-working people who do not have a big load of money. Because their focus isn't about flashy cash – their focus is on being a tight-knit family and spending time together and just being their authentic selves.

So, for her mother-in-law to spend $325 so that her daughter-in-law could run the show in the kitchen – that's an outward sign of her mother-in-law saying to her that they care, and they want her to have it good.

She had fun at the store choosing whatever foods she wanted to have at her mother-in-law's generous expense. Think about it – she was getting attention – she was in control, right?

Everybody was getting along just fine. She and the girls were happy and relaxed and enjoying the

MISS MENSA'S THEORY ~ on the Case of Christopher Watts Specific to Family Violence and Child Abuse is an opinion essay written to explore whether Christopher Watts is guilty of murdering his wife and their daughters beyond all reasonable doubt.

time they were spending with the girls' Mimi and Papa.

And then suddenly when she was no longer the center of attention, all hell broke loose.

They weren't expecting to babysit their other grandchildren. They were spending time with their son's wife and children. And everything was calm.

But when their daughter called and asked if she could drop the kids off because she was called into work, everything changed.

She got quiet. She knew her sister-in-law was on her way. And then literally within minutes of her sister-in-law dropping her children off and heading off to work – seriously all hell broke loose.

Nobody put Bella and Ce Ce in any danger at all. And nobody in their entire family ever would – the

MISS MENSA'S THEORY ~ on the Case of Christopher Watts Specific to Family Violence and Child Abuse is an opinion essay written to explore whether Christopher Watts is guilty of murdering his wife and their daughters beyond all reasonable doubt.

Watts family loved Bella and Ce Ce and their mother too, of course.

But evidently, their mother didn't love watching her sister-in-law scurry off to her successful career after hugging her parents and her children goodbye. I think that she wanted to be just like her sister-in-law. But, she didn't know how.

Because after the "other grandchildren", as she called her sister-in-law's children, arrived at Mimi and Papa's house, the kids lined up for ice cream, which is a perfectly normal routine for kids heading to their grandparents' house, right?

Mrs. Watts set the kids up at the table and clearly instructed them to sit right at the table with their ice cream and then to wash their hands well before they played with Bella and Ce Ce after their treat. You see "the other grandchildren" were not eating ice cream that was on their aunties approved shopping list. So, in deference to her daughter-in-law's ridiculous

MISS MENSA'S THEORY ~ on the Case of Christopher Watts Specific to Family Violence and Child Abuse is an opinion essay written to explore whether Christopher Watts is guilty of murdering his wife and their daughters beyond all reasonable doubt.

claims, Mimi told the kids to sit right at that table with their treat.

Remember that the fridge and the freezer were both chuck full of food for Bella and Ce Ce from the big shopping trip. THERE WAS SPECIAL ICE CREAM FOR THEM RIGHT IN THE FREEZER.

If their mom wanted them to have ice-cream, it was right there in the freezer for her to serve the girls ice-cream from her approved list of foods the girls could eat.

But instead of scooping ice-cream for the girls, she had a scream-fest instead. While her mother-in-law was tending to her "other grandchildren", she chose to explode.

Why?

Why didn't she ask the girls if they wanted ice-cream and then go serve it up for them?

Instead, she accused her in-laws of trying to harm Bella and Ce Ce.

MISS MENSA'S THEORY ~ on the Case of Christopher Watts Specific to Family Violence and Child Abuse is an opinion essay written to explore whether Christopher Watts is guilty of murdering his wife and their daughters beyond all reasonable doubt.

I think that seeing her sister-in-law and then watching her mother-in-law and "the other grandchildren" was too much for her to handle.

If you pay attention to the insults that are being hurled toward her in-laws on social media, it's interesting to note what they are saying is proof that "they didn't love her and the girls as much as they loved their daughter and her children".

No kidding.

The attackers say that his dad had a tattoo with the other grandchildren's names. That they gave the other grandchildren ice-cream but not Bella and Ce Ce? That they were closer to their other grandchildren?

What?

That's absurd!

They no doubt love all their grandchildren with all their hearts. But consider the accusations –

MISS MENSA'S THEORY ~ on the Case of Christopher Watts Specific to Family Violence and Child Abuse is an opinion essay written to explore whether Christopher Watts is guilty of murdering his wife and their daughters beyond all reasonable doubt.

better than? Less than? That isn't how it works, folks.

I think that she was jealous of his sister from the day they met. And I think that seeing his sister that day and seeing her children and her in-laws in action once again made her feel "less than" not because of anything at all that his parents said or did, but because I think that his wife just simply didn't know how to feel like she really belonged, or how to be authentic herself, or perhaps how to not be the center of attention?

Just listen to some of what she said about the meltdown - "live or die"?

"Never step foot in their house again"?

"Deathly allergic"? "Severely anaphylactic"? And then the coup de gras was when she told her mother-in-law a big "F.U." on social media. That pretty much says it all right then and there after she texted ad nauseum that her mother-in-law gave her "other grandchildren" ice cream.

MISS MENSA'S THEORY ~ on the Case of Christopher Watts Specific to Family Violence and Child Abuse is an opinion essay written to explore whether Christopher Watts is guilty of murdering his wife and their daughters beyond all reasonable doubt.

Consider the distancing language she used in her rants about the meltdown – she called her nieces and nephews "the other grandchildren" and she called her sister-in-law "her daughter". That isn't normal. That's someone who is distant and insecure.

And the result of her nut meltdown is interesting too – she was shaking. She was angry. She was yelling. She was accusing them of not caring if their own grandchildren lived or died.

They ran out the door. And when they dared to return TO THEIR OWN HOME, she was still shaking, and angry, and yelling at them.

She dialed her dad and told him to pick her and the girls up saying the girls would never step foot in their house again. And just one month later poor little Bella and Ce Ce were dead.

I think she really wanted what her husband had – or to be more specific – I think she wanted what her husband's sister had - a solid beginning with

MISS MENSA'S THEORY ~ on the Case of Christopher Watts Specific to Family Violence and Child Abuse is an opinion essay written to explore whether Christopher Watts is guilty of murdering his wife and their daughters beyond all reasonable doubt.

the same home since birth, the relatives close-by, the life-long friends, the goals, the determination - but I don't think she knew how to get it - except by taking it from those around her, like a chameleon?

Or maybe by taking it from her husband, like a parasite.

But that isn't the only reason that I think she felt insecure around his family, especially around his sister. I think the other problem she had besides feeling "less than" around her in-laws was that she was afraid that her in-laws and his friends would be able to see right through her.

The sad part is that she could have just been herself around them and they would have loved and accepted her just fine. But I don't think she knew about unconditional love. I think she lived her life fearful of being "less than".

It's interesting that in her death, the people who are discussing the case online who are calling her

MISS MENSA'S THEORY ~ on the Case of Christopher Watts Specific to Family Violence and Child Abuse is an opinion essay written to explore whether Christopher Watts is guilty of murdering his wife and their daughters beyond all reasonable doubt.

a saint and saying how perfect she was, seem to be perpetuating that superficial struggle that it appears she dealt with in her life. When people expect her to be superhuman after her death, then how was she expected to be while she was still alive? Perfect? Hard-working? Successful? Yet, was she ever perfect, hard-working, or successful at all?

There's another sad issue that I think she faced which is rarely addressed in the case discussion groups on social media – I think that she was an extremely fearful person.

I first started to wonder about just how fearful she seemed when I noticed how fearful the children were.

Watch the videos.

Santa Claus was right in their own home? And they were both screaming in fear? At Santa's house, okay, that makes sense. But when Santa is

MISS MENSA'S THEORY ~ on the Case of Christopher Watts Specific to Family Violence and Child Abuse is an opinion essay written to explore whether Christopher Watts is guilty of murdering his wife and their daughters beyond all reasonable doubt.

right in their own home and their mom is right there with them, why were they so afraid?

The most heartbreaking example of course was when poor little Bella talked to the babysitter about being afraid that she would never see her sister again if Ce Ce ate coconut.

Did you know that both girls were deathly afraid of dirt? That's right. They were too afraid of dirt to touch it.

Did you know they were afraid of animals?

Did you notice how we're told they SCREAMED if their mother was absent?

In my opinion, it's obvious that Christopher Watts' wife expected to always be in total control. As I stated earlier, I think she used her claims of illnesses, diseases, and allergies too, in order to get attention and to gain and to maintain total control.

MISS MENSA'S THEORY ~ on the Case of Christopher Watts Specific to Family Violence and Child Abuse is an opinion essay written to explore whether Christopher Watts is guilty of murdering his wife and their daughters beyond all reasonable doubt.

Well, when someone is a total control freak, it makes sense that their need for total control stems from some deeply rooted fears.

And sadly, I think she was not only playing out her special brand of medical madness by using her children (perhaps as the patients the wannabe nurse would never have), but I think she was serving up fear to her children on such a regular basis that both girls were becoming fearful themselves.

Back to the chameleon, or more precisely, the parasitic approach to her relationship with Christopher Watts. I think she wanted what he had. But instead of standing by his side and watching and learning, like a chameleon - I think she latched onto him like a parasite and began sucking him dry – his finances, his savings account, his time, his energy, his ideas, his goals – and with their blurred boundaries, I think his identity was soon lost and sadly replaced by a

MISS MENSA'S THEORY ~ on the Case of Christopher Watts Specific to Family Violence and Child Abuse is an opinion essay written to explore whether Christopher Watts is guilty of murdering his wife and their daughters beyond all reasonable doubt.

toxic blend of both of their personalities wrapped in one.

I'm not saying at all that Christopher Watts was perfect or that she in any way deserved to die. I am saying however that Christopher Watts and his family were solid, hard-working people who were respectful of others. They were and are honest people who trust others without realizing there are cons and crooks in the world just waiting to take advantage of them. And it's from that place of naivete that Christopher Watts was born.

I think when their two personalities morphed into a toxic blend that his wife was the dominant personality and his was basically stifled into oblivion.

Except when it was time to take family photos.

She needed him in order to play out her charade. Well, she needed his income stream anyway. And

MISS MENSA'S THEORY ~ on the Case of Christopher Watts Specific to Family Violence and Child Abuse is an opinion essay written to explore whether Christopher Watts is guilty of murdering his wife and their daughters beyond all reasonable doubt.

she needed him to do as he was told and then to smile big for the camera.

When the toxic blend took over, in his place was the shell of the man he was when he met her - while she promoted herself to the position of being the host to his supposed parasitic ways.

He was fat? He was dumb? He was not her type?

Examine the reversal - he had a good job, a savings account, excellent credit, and he completed post high school education too.

He was intelligent. He was fit. He had a loving family and life-long friends. He knew how to set goals and how to work hard, ACTUALLY WORK HARD, to achieve them.

At the time of her death, after just a six-year-long marriage, the narrative on the case reads that she was a highly successful employee of a billion dollar MLM who was raking in the big

MISS MENSA'S THEORY ~ on the Case of Christopher Watts Specific to Family Violence and Child Abuse is an opinion essay written to explore whether Christopher Watts is guilty of murdering his wife and their daughters beyond all reasonable doubt.

money, that she had her college degree, that she was a nurse, that she was so intelligent, and fit, and that she was such a great mom too.

Now take a closer look at who the narrative does describe - both Christopher Watts when he met her, and her sister-in-law too.

I think that his wife struggled with her own identity issues - and her own sense of self-worth. And sadly, when she met him, I think she needed him to lose his own identity, and to hand it right over to her.

Which brings us to the major flaw in his personality - he was a doormat. He was timid. He was so trusting of others that he refused to see the obvious signs of trouble.

He stood by and allowed his daughter to be sprayed right in the face while he did nothing to save her.

MISS MENSA'S THEORY ~ on the Case of Christopher Watts Specific to Family Violence and Child Abuse is an opinion essay written to explore whether Christopher Watts is guilty of murdering his wife and their daughters beyond all reasonable doubt.

He stood by and watched both of his daughters scream high to the heavens when he was wearing the Santa Claus suit and they were scared and looking for him. Even though his wife was right there - the girls were both literally petrified. He should have ripped off that stupid costume and comforted his children. But he didn't. Because there was a video to make and he didn't dare to not to exactly as he was told to do - by his wife.

He didn't stand up to his wife. For that alone, he is guilty.

MISS MENSA'S THEORY ~ on the Case of Christopher Watts Specific to Family Violence and Child Abuse is an opinion essay written to explore whether Christopher Watts is guilty of murdering his wife and their daughters beyond all reasonable doubt.

Progressive Dehumanization

Abusers do not have flashing neon signs on their foreheads that read "I'm an abuser".

They start out nice. Then they start to isolate you from your friends and family members. Then they start to blur the boundaries in the relationship making it easy for them to begin to work toward depriving you of your own identity.

It isn't sudden. It isn't obvious. It takes time.

But before long, the abuser is successful in basically dehumanizing you.

You become an object.

You become their appendage.

You become their tool.

MISS MENSA'S THEORY ~ on the Case of Christopher Watts Specific to Family Violence and Child Abuse is an opinion essay written to explore whether Christopher Watts is guilty of murdering his wife and their daughters beyond all reasonable doubt.

And you become their excuse for acting the way they do.

Christopher Watts' wife was very demeaning toward her husband, especially evidenced by her text messages to her "friends" toward the end of her life. She bashed him big time then said it was time to go masturbate. To her husband she was saying she wanted to save their marriage. To her "friends" she was treating both her husband, and his family, with absolute disrespect.

To his face, she called him "dummy". To his own parents even, she ridiculed his looks, his actions, his job, his car, you name it and she ridiculed it.

To his friends, she expected him to distance himself.

To his sister? She seemed to expect for his sister to simply disappear.

Right along with his parents.

MISS MENSA'S THEORY ~ on the Case of Christopher Watts Specific to Family Violence and Child Abuse is an opinion essay written to explore whether Christopher Watts is guilty of murdering his wife and their daughters beyond all reasonable doubt.

And then she sounded confused right at the end of her life why he was leaving her.

And she asked him whether he would stay if they didn't have kids.

Compare that behavior with how she behaved when they first met. Remember, she wanted to have ten children. She thought he had a great job. She thought his Mustang was cool.

But then, before long, she was laughing at him when he freaked out because his car was sitting out in the driveway during a hailstorm.

She thought it was funny.

Because by then my hunch is that she no longer viewed him as a person at all.

Abusers will keep their victim exhausted. And I think that's what happened in his case. Because I think he was just too tired, especially after the children came along, to realize how poorly he was being treated.

MISS MENSA'S THEORY ~ on the Case of Christopher Watts Specific to Family Violence and Child Abuse is an opinion essay written to explore whether Christopher Watts is guilty of murdering his wife and their daughters beyond all reasonable doubt.

I don't think at the end of their marriage that she viewed him as a person at all. I think she viewed him as a paycheck. As her way of having the house she wanted. As her way of being able to present herself as a successful entrepreneur when, in fact, I think she was using his earnings and her charge cards to make it appear as if she was successful.

Watch the video where they're playing life-size checkers. She is sitting on the phone while she's telling him where to move. And she calls him a loser.

While he does as he's told and moves wherever she tells him to in much the same way he appears to do in real life. That life size checkers video is an interesting illustration, in my opinion, of the true dynamic of their marriage. She even says in one video that "Chris will do whatever (she) tells him to do.

MISS MENSA'S THEORY ~ on the Case of Christopher Watts Specific to Family Violence and Child Abuse is an opinion essay written to explore whether Christopher Watts is guilty of murdering his wife and their daughters beyond all reasonable doubt.

During the couple's two-year courtship, I think progressive dehumanization had already occurred to the point that he was a mere object in her eyes, no longer a person, but a way for her to get what she evidently thought she needed to get – the house, the kids, the car, the appearance of success.

And then by the time the kids were born I think he was also feeling like he was basically no longer a person, with his own ideas, and goals, and opinions.

They were blurred into one identity – hers – and he took his position as the provider while he seemingly failed to any longer expect anything at all from the relationship – except to hopefully make her happy so she wouldn't explode on him again.

It's important to know that Christopher Watts didn't walk when she told him to do something – he ran.

MISS MENSA'S THEORY ~ on the Case of Christopher Watts Specific to Family Violence and Child Abuse is an opinion essay written to explore whether Christopher Watts is guilty of murdering his wife and their daughters beyond all reasonable doubt.

As if he was frantic to please her.

As if maybe he was afraid of her if he didn't do move fast enough to do whatever it was she was telling him to do.

MISS MENSA'S THEORY ~ on the Case of Christopher Watts Specific to Family Violence and Child Abuse is an opinion essay written to explore whether Christopher Watts is guilty of murdering his wife and their daughters beyond all reasonable doubt.

Financial Abuse

In my opinion, their marriage was already over back in March of 2018 when Christopher Watts found out that his wife had not made the mortgage payments for the last three months straight.

Remember that we're told she was a huge financial success as an entrepreneur for MLMs she was promoting. But she wasn't. Because they were flat broke. I think she was lying to him every step of the way when it came to their finances.

She convinced him that he was a real "Dummy" when it came to handling money and that since she was highly skilled in handling finances then she would take over. Oh, she was highly skilled,

MISS MENSA'S THEORY ~ on the Case of Christopher Watts Specific to Family Violence and Child Abuse is an opinion essay written to explore whether Christopher Watts is guilty of murdering his wife and their daughters beyond all reasonable doubt.

alright. But I think what she was highly skilled at had more to do with conning people than it did with knowing how to pay the bills.

In March of 2018, Christopher Watts had to take 10k out of his 401k in order to save their home.

Then she spoke with a lawyer about divorce and custody.

And then she announced that she was pregnant.

Talk about convenient timing.

Her husband catches her not paying the mortgage payments for three months straight and boom - she gets pregnant?

Remember that when he met her, he was financially sound. Then he bought the house on his own without her on the mortgage at all. And then, just one month later, he quit-claim deeded interest in the house to her. And then, just a couple of years later, the bankruptcy debts were discharged to the tune of 70k. Yep, she was

MISS MENSA'S THEORY ~ on the Case of Christopher Watts Specific to Family Violence and Child Abuse is an opinion essay written to explore whether Christopher Watts is guilty of murdering his wife and their daughters beyond all reasonable doubt.

highly skilled with handling the family finances, alright.

Here is what I was told just the other day by a woman who called me with information about "the dining room table". In over thirteen months of discussing this case, I had yet to hear anything about what people are referring to as the "dining room table scam". But this is what I've been told - and based on the other lies we've been told about how successful (and physically ill), Christopher Watts' wife was, I absolutely think it's reasonable to believe this story about the dining room table is true.

People who knew the couple knew they had a beautiful dining room table. Suddenly, the dining room table was gone. They were confused as to why she no longer wanted her beautiful dining room table and had replaced it with one that wasn't nearly as nice and was presumably much less expensive. She told them that she didn't like

MISS MENSA'S THEORY ~ on the Case of Christopher Watts Specific to Family Violence and Child Abuse is an opinion essay written to explore whether Christopher Watts is guilty of murdering his wife and their daughters beyond all reasonable doubt.

her dining room table anymore, so she decided to replace it.

But the story goes that she bought the nice dining room table right before they filed for bankruptcy in 2015. The story goes that she bought the nice dining room table on credit with the intention of including the debt in the bankruptcy filing – in order to basically get her very expensive dining room table for free.

But it didn't work out for her quite as she planned. Because the dining room table was repossessed. And after it was repossessed and she replaced it with the lower priced table, that's when she explained that she just didn't like the other table anymore.

Of course, she left out the part about how her plan to discharge the debt in the bankruptcy hadn't worked out for her when the creditor appeared suddenly at her door to repossess it. It was there one day and gone the next. And then it

MISS MENSA'S THEORY ~ on the Case of Christopher Watts Specific to Family Violence and Child Abuse is an opinion essay written to explore whether Christopher Watts is guilty of murdering his wife and their daughters beyond all reasonable doubt.

was replaced by one that was not nearly as expensive or nice. Yep, that's a successful businesswoman alright.

How disgusting, seriously, for a person to abuse the bankruptcy system like that. Equally disgusting is the official narrative on the case which claims that she had to file a bankruptcy due to all her medical bills stemming from all her alleged diseases. Baloney. Look at the bankruptcy docs. If she had to file a bankruptcy due to medical bills then it appears that both Macy's and JCP are now medical service providers.

Consider the timeline – she meets Christopher Watts. She quits her job. She convinces him to sell his car, to move 1,600 miles away from family and friends and his high-paying job. She convinces him to buy the brand-new house on his own and to add her name one month later to the deed.

She convinces him they need to file bankruptcy. And then she keeps right on spending as if she

MISS MENSA'S THEORY ~ on the Case of Christopher Watts Specific to Family Violence and Child Abuse is an opinion essay written to explore whether Christopher Watts is guilty of murdering his wife and their daughters beyond all reasonable doubt.

thinks money does grow on trees. She dabbles in MLMs and convinces her husband that she's raking in 65k per year. While she can't even make the house payments. She convinces her husband that she "earned" a Lexus from being SOOO successful as an MLM promoter. And somehow, she also convinced him to sign the lease documents for the free car. In June of 2018, the court documents arrived regarding the unpaid HOA dues totaling over 1,500 dollars. Be clear, they were being sued for not paying just $1,500. Their court date was looming, scheduled to occur just one week after the children were murdered. When they received the court docs, did she pay the bill immediately? After all, she was making 65k per year, right?

No, instead she convinced her husband that it was all just a big mistake because she suddenly realized she had been mailing the payments for the HOA dues to the wrong address all along. And he believed her. Obviously, if she was mailing the

MISS MENSA'S THEORY ~ on the Case of Christopher Watts Specific to Family Violence and Child Abuse is an opinion essay written to explore whether Christopher Watts is guilty of murdering his wife and their daughters beyond all reasonable doubt.

payments to the wrong address for the last year or year and a half then the money would have still been in their account, right? And obviously, had she been mailing the payments to the wrong address the HOA would have contacted her before ever filing suit against them, right? Oh, wait. Maybe the HOA did contact her. And maybe that's why she was always very careful to never allow Christopher Watts to ever see any of their mail.

While she was in North Carolina for five weeks before he joined her and the kids for the sixth and final week of their "vacation", she had her friend pick up the mail from their house. He was home. He owned the house. He was supporting the family from day one. And he wasn't allowed to see his own mail? I think that while she was in North Carolina that he did catch a glimpse of her messy "office". And I think he realized, maybe for the first time in their relationship, that she had been lying to him all along.

MISS MENSA'S THEORY ~ on the Case of Christopher Watts Specific to Family Violence and Child Abuse is an opinion essay written to explore whether Christopher Watts is guilty of murdering his wife and their daughters beyond all reasonable doubt.

I think she was using credit cards to make it appear as if she was earning an income. And I think she was purposely keeping them broke in order to try to make it financially impossible for him to leave.

But for Christopher Watts, as broke as they were and as trapped as he may have felt for years already, I think he was finally catching on to the financial disaster his wife seemed to be creating – again. And I think he finally mustered up the guts to say ENOUGH. Not because of the money alone, and not because of the way she seemed to be keeping the girls sick, and not because of any girlfriend. I think he wanted to leave her because – of her and her alone.

I think that Christopher Watts was finally tired of her nonsense. I think he was tired of being her slave. I think he was tired of hearing about her long list of ailments. And I think he worried about their children's health and wondered if what she

MISS MENSA'S THEORY ~ on the Case of Christopher Watts Specific to Family Violence and Child Abuse is an opinion essay written to explore whether Christopher Watts is guilty of murdering his wife and their daughters beyond all reasonable doubt.

was telling him and the doctors about their children's health problems was true. I think he was tired of taking her orders. But what I think he was most tired of – at the end of their marriage – was her incessant rants about how terrible she thought his family was. He had enough. He was beginning to see right through her – as it appears his family members had been able to do right from the start. He was beginning to say no to her. He was beginning to see her for who she really was – a woman perhaps that he didn't trust, or admire, or love.

MISS MENSA'S THEORY ~ on the Case of Christopher Watts Specific to Family Violence and Child Abuse is an opinion essay written to explore whether Christopher Watts is guilty of murdering his wife and their daughters beyond all reasonable doubt.

Munchausen by Proxy

So, we've learned so far that it's quite possible, and reasonable to believe based on the autopsy reports and her ever-changing stories, that she was never sick to begin with.

That's right.

When a person claims they are taking 26 pills a day and they can magically stop taking those pills because the weather helped with 95% of her diseases, then common sense dictates there's a whole lot of lying going on.

And we've learned that it seems rather obvious she was doing her best to isolate her husband from his family members and his life-long friends.

We've learned that after paying closing costs it's likely she never made a dime on the house she claimed she made big money on.

MISS MENSA'S THEORY ~ on the Case of Christopher Watts Specific to Family Violence and Child Abuse is an opinion essay written to explore whether Christopher Watts is guilty of murdering his wife and their daughters beyond all reasonable doubt.

And we've learned that the bankruptcy was not at all about medical bills unless Macy's and JCP are now providing medical services.

We've learned that she was divorced before meeting Christopher Watts.

And just the other day I received the screenshot of a comment she posted in a "survivor of spousal abuse" support group on Facebook where she said she was SCARED because she was in love with another man and it would take "drastic measures" for her to be with the man she belonged with.

Survivor of spousal abuse?

Really?

We've learned that she was never a nurse and that she never graduated from college either.

In fact, it sounds like she barely made it through just one term. We've learned to question whether she was in a nursing program at all, even for just that one term because according to the school

MISS MENSA'S THEORY ~ on the Case of Christopher Watts Specific to Family Violence and Child Abuse is an opinion essay written to explore whether Christopher Watts is guilty of murdering his wife and their daughters beyond all reasonable doubt.

she claimed accepted her into their nursing program, the program she claimed that she was enrolled in likely never existed. Could it be she was taking entry level classes for one term at the university? Likely so.

We've learned that she said she lost her friends when she told them about all of her "health challenges".

And we've learned that she made new friends online.

We've learned that she called herself a stay-at-home mom even though while she was staying at home - both children were in daycare.

Yes, we've learned a lot about the case of Christopher Watts since it first hit the headline news back in August of 2018.

And we've also learned there is an organized group trying to silence us from being ALLOWED to discuss the case.

MISS MENSA'S THEORY ~ on the Case of Christopher Watts Specific to Family Violence and Child Abuse is an opinion essay written to explore whether Christopher Watts is guilty of murdering his wife and their daughters beyond all reasonable doubt.

We've learned from the attackers that it seems everything they are accusing us of seems to apply to the woman they call their "saint".

So, it follows that when the attackers accuse us of being child abusers, that we are digging into the details of the case to see what it is that they appear to be trying to hide about Christopher Watts' wife.

And after digging into the details of the case, I believe she was medically abusing poor little Bella and Ce Ce, perhaps since the day they were born.

I've been told by reliable sources, and I think it's reasonable to believe that what I've been told is true, that there was an open CPS case against her when she died which required that she not be alone with the children,

that she was not allowed to take the children to the doctor, or for any medical care at any medical care facility, and that both girls were to be placed in daycare while their father was at work.

MISS MENSA'S THEORY ~ on the Case of Christopher Watts Specific to Family Violence and Child Abuse is an opinion essay written to explore whether Christopher Watts is guilty of murdering his wife and their daughters beyond all reasonable doubt.

I've been told that if the girls were not in daycare at opening time, then the authorities were to be contacted.

And I was told the reason for the open CPS case was that she was caught medically abusing both children right at the hospital in December of 2016.

Think about it – why on earth were the girls both in daycare while she was claiming to be a stay-at-home mom?

She was busy working?

Really?

Because it sounded like the extent of her working was to mail out free samples, make videos to tell everybody how excited she was, and to head off on those "free" vacations while her husband stayed home with the kids.

Also, remember that in the discovery documents we learned there was a caseworker in North

---

MISS MENSA'S THEORY ~ on the Case of Christopher Watts Specific to Family Violence and Child Abuse is an opinion essay written to explore whether Christopher Watts is guilty of murdering his wife and their daughters beyond all reasonable doubt.

Carolina who wanted a call back from the investigators.

It seems obvious that if there was a caseworker in North Carolina with information on the case, then what I'm being told is true since the people who are contacting me are insisting that while they were in North Carolina that their case was transferred to North Carolina for supervision.

Also, consider the number of times that Bella and Ce Ce were subjected to medical appointments, tests, procedures, treatments, etc.

Did you know that poor little Bella and Ce Ce were getting their temps taken daily?

Do you know how their mother took their temps?

With a rectal thermometer.

Their medical appointments seemed to be constant and never-ending – one right after another – with those poor girls looking sad or in pain or uncomfortable in the photos their mother

MISS MENSA'S THEORY ~ on the Case of Christopher Watts Specific to Family Violence and Child Abuse is an opinion essay written to explore whether Christopher Watts is guilty of murdering his wife and their daughters beyond all reasonable doubt.

posted on social media – while she sat there with a big smile on her face.

She was especially excited when she finally found a doctor who would perform surgery on both girls.

Seriously, what kind of mother is happy that two preschool age little girls will both be getting tubes in their ears on the same day?

And how many doctors did they see before she "finally found" one who would agree with her that the girls needed tubes? How many doctors did the girls have to see while she was trying to get them diagnosed with FAMILIAL MEDITERRANEAN FEVER?

How many doctors did they have to see while she was trying to convince them that both girls were "severely anaphylactic" and "deathly allergic" to common foods?

Were the girls sick?

MISS MENSA'S THEORY ~ on the Case of Christopher Watts Specific to Family Violence and Child Abuse is an opinion essay written to explore whether Christopher Watts is guilty of murdering his wife and their daughters beyond all reasonable doubt.

Were the girls really suffering from breathing problems?

Were they really suffering from Familial Mediterranean Fever?

Were they allergic to any foods at all?

Typically, a parent who is medically abusing their child(ren) is the mother. And typically, the child(ren) who are being medically abused, are preschool age.

Parents who are medically abusing their child(ren) often use Facebook to carry out their attention seeking antics where they can get the attention that they crave without being found out for the bad acts they are committing.

Look at the video where she claims she gave the girls amoxicillin, prednisone, and LOTS OF TYLENOL.

Look at the video where she says both girls were at the emergency room the night before – she

MISS MENSA'S THEORY ~ on the Case of Christopher Watts Specific to Family Violence and Child Abuse is an opinion essay written to explore whether Christopher Watts is guilty of murdering his wife and their daughters beyond all reasonable doubt.

said one had viral pneumonia and she couldn't remember what the other one had but she'd just have to get through it.

And again, most alarming is her Facebook post where she says she's so happy because she finally found a doctor who will perform surgery on both girls.

Look at all her posts about allergies, and asthma, and stomach problems too.

And seriously, why on earth is she taking their temps daily with a rectal thermometer? This is not normal, folks. Not at all. Rectal thermometers are seriously outdated and were only used for tiny infants even back in the day when they were still used. But poor little Bella and Ce Ce were subjected to having their temps taken rectally daily at ages three and almost five? For what? So that their mother could try to convince the specialists that they had FAMILIAL MEDITERRANEAN FEVER?

MISS MENSA'S THEORY ~ on the Case of Christopher Watts Specific to Family Violence and Child Abuse is an opinion essay written to explore whether Christopher Watts is guilty of murdering his wife and their daughters beyond all reasonable doubt.

Those poor babies had stomach problems from the start.

They had procedures, and surgeries, and medications, and breathing treatments, and you name it and they had it. Why?

Remember that according to the autopsies that both girls, and their mother, were healthy. But it appears their own mother was making, and keeping, them sick.

And Christopher Watts believed every word that his wife told him about their "sick" children. Isn't it interesting that over one year after their deaths that we're now being told he wants his children's medical records to be sealed?

Could it be that he is recognizing the possibility that his wife was lying to him all along?

If she was lying to him about their children's "illnesses" he was in good company because tragically it appears that at least one or two

MISS MENSA'S THEORY ~ on the Case of Christopher Watts Specific to Family Violence and Child Abuse is an opinion essay written to explore whether Christopher Watts is guilty of murdering his wife and their daughters beyond all reasonable doubt.

doctors also believed her claims every step of the way.

Consider her excited Facebook post about how happy she was to finally find a doctor who would perform surgery on both girls in the same day.

Did you know that within one week of learning that Christopher Watts had a blocked tear duct when he was a baby that suddenly his wife was claiming that one of the girls had a blocked tear duct too? Isn't that just so coincidental? But, of course, how on earth could someone cause a tear duct to be blocked? Or could it be that it wasn't really blocked at all?

Did you know that within one week of hearing about another dog with some sort of spinal issue that the family dog suddenly had a spinal issue too?

That post was interesting – it sounded like the "disease" was diagnosed and the treatment plan

MISS MENSA'S THEORY ~ on the Case of Christopher Watts Specific to Family Violence and Child Abuse is an opinion essay written to explore whether Christopher Watts is guilty of murdering his wife and their daughters beyond all reasonable doubt.

for the dog was already taking place before x-rays were even taken.

There was a bit of confusion over the FAMILIAL MEDITERRANEAN FEVER claims too. At one point she posted that one of the girls was diagnosed with FMF but then three months later it sounded like the specialists were "leaning toward" that diagnosis.

Did you know that according to the Mayo Clinic website that the three most common illnesses that children who are being medically abused have are -

1.) breathing problems,

2.) stomach problems, and

3.) allergies.

And guess what – poor little Bella and Ce Ce, according to their mother anyway, had all the above.

MISS MENSA'S THEORY ~ on the Case of Christopher Watts Specific to Family Violence and Child Abuse is an opinion essay written to explore whether Christopher Watts is guilty of murdering his wife and their daughters beyond all reasonable doubt.

And the three most common methods that parents who are medically abusing their children use are –

1.) poisoning (syrup of ipecac, dish soap, very hot spices, etc.),

2.) malnutrition (check out the video where Bella is saying she's hungry and then she starts to cry while her mother eats right in front of her), and

3.) smothering.

Bella and Ce Ce were both smothered the night they were murdered by one of their parents in what should have been the safety of their own home.

Let that sink in.

MISS MENSA'S THEORY ~ on the Case of Christopher Watts Specific to Family Violence and Child Abuse is an opinion essay written to explore whether Christopher Watts is guilty of murdering his wife and their daughters beyond all reasonable doubt.

Was There an Open CPS Case?

Remember the message for the investigators left by a caseworker from North Carolina that was in the discovery documents.

Why?

Why would a caseworker from North Carolina be wanting to speak with investigators working on a case in Colorado?

Well, it makes sense to me that if there was an open CPS case then, while she and the girls were in North Carolina, the case would have had to have been transferred during their stay.

Right?

I have been contacted by what I believe are reliable sources and I think it is reasonable to believe them when they tell me there was an open CPS case against Christopher Watts' wife.

And I'll tell you why.

MISS MENSA'S THEORY ~ on the Case of Christopher Watts Specific to Family Violence and Child Abuse is an opinion essay written to explore whether Christopher Watts is guilty of murdering his wife and their daughters beyond all reasonable doubt.

I do not believe his wife was an honest person.

I think the attempts to rewrite her "reputation" have led many of us who have been unfairly harassed, stalked, bullied, doxed, threatened, slandered, defamed, and libeled to conclude in fact that she was nothing short of a con.

I do not believe that she was intelligent or successful either.

In fact, I do not even believe that she was sane. Because I think that at the time of her death that she had some serious issues going on.

And I think that one of her issues was that she was under heavy scrutiny and supervision specific to her parenting skills by CPS.

I'll be blunt.

After researching the details of this case and watching the abusive tactics used by the attackers who seem hell-bent on hiding the facts of this case, including their accusations against

MISS MENSA'S THEORY ~ on the Case of Christopher Watts Specific to Family Violence and Child Abuse is an opinion essay written to explore whether Christopher Watts is guilty of murdering his wife and their daughters beyond all reasonable doubt.

those of us they are attacking that we are child abusers, combined with the calls I have received from people who sound sincere, intelligent, and well-spoken regarding whether there was an open CPS case at the time of her death – I believe it's reasonable, plausible, and downright probable that it's true.

I do believe that she was medically abusing poor little Bella and Ce Ce. And I do believe that she was under supervision of CPS.

I also believe that part of the reason for her desperate attempts to "save" her marriage right at the end was because in the event the couple did divorce, which I believe was about to occur - given the antics over the summer combined with the financial issues - that Christopher Watts' wife was desperate to "save" the marriage in order to keep her secrets hidden.

Hear me out – if there was an open CPS case, and I believe it is reasonable to believe there was,

MISS MENSA'S THEORY ~ on the Case of Christopher Watts Specific to Family Violence and Child Abuse is an opinion essay written to explore whether Christopher Watts is guilty of murdering his wife and their daughters beyond all reasonable doubt.

then when the couple divorced, that secret would become known, right?

Do you think she would have gotten custody of the children?

I don't.

Do you think she would have been able to afford to continue promoting her MLM products?

I don't.

Do you think she would have been able to afford the house on her own?

I don't.

Do you think she would have been able to keep the Lexus?

I don't.

Do you think she would have been able to continue to enjoy all of those "free" vacations?

I don't.

MISS MENSA'S THEORY ~ on the Case of Christopher Watts Specific to Family Violence and Child Abuse is an opinion essay written to explore whether Christopher Watts is guilty of murdering his wife and their daughters beyond all reasonable doubt.

What if when she spoke with the lawyer, back in late March or early April, she learned that Christopher Watts may have been able to get permission to move back to North Carolina?

Could that help explain the nut meltdown in July?

What if she learned she might have to pay child support? Or have supervised visits? Or that she might have to face Christopher Watts being able to visit his family with the girls any time he damn well wanted to with or without her permission?

What if she realized that he had a girlfriend and she worried that they were more serious about each other than perhaps they really were?

Could it be that she simply couldn't handle the thought of the girls spending time with his girlfriend?

Could it be that she simply couldn't handle the thought of not being able to continue micromanaging his life?

MISS MENSA'S THEORY ~ on the Case of Christopher Watts Specific to Family Violence and Child Abuse is an opinion essay written to explore whether Christopher Watts is guilty of murdering his wife and their daughters beyond all reasonable doubt.

What if – in a divorce – suddenly the girls were totally healthy? Seriously, what if? If it is true that she was medically abusing the children, then surely their health would have improved had he divorced her and been awarded custody, right?

I think that it's quite possible she was not about to allow any of her secrets to ever be revealed.

So, think it through - if there was an open CPS case at the time of her death then, in my opinion, she should have been considered the number one suspect in the murders of poor little Bella and Ce Ce, whether she survived.

And this, my friends, in my opinion, is the big secret that the attackers who are trying to silence us are trying to hide.

I think she was medically abusing the children.

And I think that smothering them was nothing new.

MISS MENSA'S THEORY ~ on the Case of Christopher Watts Specific to Family Violence and Child Abuse is an opinion essay written to explore whether Christopher Watts is guilty of murdering his wife and their daughters beyond all reasonable doubt.

Look at the "photo op" video posted on my bitchute.com channel. In one photo after another the babies are sleeping with their heads totally covered by heavy blankets or full-size pillows.

That is not normal at all.

Look at how often both girls were sick.

Again, that isn't normal at all.

Look at how excited she was to find a doctor who would perform surgery on both girls.

Again, that is not normal at all.

How many glaring bits of evidence that she was medically abusing Bella and Ce Ce do we need to see before we admit that it sure does appear that she was harming those poor little girls from day one?

How many glaring bits of evidence do we need to see before we catch a clue that it is possible that Christopher Watts was telling the truth in his

MISS MENSA'S THEORY ~ on the Case of Christopher Watts Specific to Family Violence and Child Abuse is an opinion essay written to explore whether Christopher Watts is guilty of murdering his wife and their daughters beyond all reasonable doubt.

first police interview when he said that HE DID NOT MURDER HIS CHILDREN?

MISS MENSA'S THEORY ~ on the Case of Christopher Watts Specific to Family Violence and Child Abuse is an opinion essay written to explore whether Christopher Watts is guilty of murdering his wife and their daughters beyond all reasonable doubt.

Her OTHER TWO DAUGHTERS?

One of the false accusations the attackers have made against those of us they are attacking is that we had children when we were young who we dumped off onto other people to raise.

Not one of us who are being attacked ever abandoned any of our children.

The accusations are absurd right along with all their other ridiculous allegations against us. And like all the other libelous attacks they have made against us – we turn to the case and wonder if it's true that Christopher Watts' wife is the person the attackers are really talking about.

Remember – the attackers say that we cheated on our spouses, are divorced, filed bankruptcies, lie about our careers and education, and that we're child abusers too.

MISS MENSA'S THEORY ~ on the Case of Christopher Watts Specific to Family Violence and Child Abuse is an opinion essay written to explore whether Christopher Watts is guilty of murdering his wife and their daughters beyond all reasonable doubt.

Now consider the FACTS of the case of Christopher Watts - Cheater? Divorcee'? Bankrupt? I don't know about you, but I've never had a dining room table "repossessed". She was a nurse? She had a nursing degree? She was ever accepted into a nursing program to begin with?

Child abuser? Well, consider her being so happy to have finally found a doctor who would perform surgery on both girls. Consider her practice of taking the children's temperature daily using a rectal thermometer. Watch the Photo Op Video. Watch the video about the multitude of doctor visits, illnesses, procedure, and don't forget - LOTS OF TYLENOL!

So, while the attackers make false statements about those of us they are attacking by saying now THAT WE ARE SUICIDAL AND THAT WE HAD CHILDREN THAT WE ABANDONED FOR OTHERS TO RAISE - logic dictates the attackers are once again lighting the path for us

MISS MENSA'S THEORY ~ on the Case of Christopher Watts Specific to Family Violence and Child Abuse is an opinion essay written to explore whether Christopher Watts is guilty of murdering his wife and their daughters beyond all reasonable doubt.

to see exactly what it is that they appear to be trying to hide about Christopher Watts' wife.

It's interesting to note that during her phone call to the police, Christopher Watts' wife's friend, the one who had no idea how old she was, and who also claimed she was somehow privy to whether she missed a doctor's appointment, you know the one – who claimed that Christopher Watts' wife was diabetic?

Well, during that phone call she stated very clearly that Christopher Watts' wife had a playdate scheduled that morning,

WITH HER OTHER TWO DAUGHTERS.

WHAT?

Her OTHER TWO DAUGHTERS?

The same friend also told the police that Christopher Watts' wife told her at one o'clock in the morning that "tomorrow morning is going to

MISS MENSA'S THEORY ~ on the Case of Christopher Watts Specific to Family Violence and Child Abuse is an opinion essay written to explore whether Christopher Watts is guilty of murdering his wife and their daughters beyond all reasonable doubt.

suck" because, she said, "the girls have to go to daycare".

Well, if the girls had to go to daycare, which I believe they did – based on a family plan through CPS - and she had a playdate scheduled WITH HER OTHER TWO DAUGHTERS, then it seems obvious that she did have two other daughters.

Follow along – the girls, Bella and Ce Ce were supposed to be in daycare that morning AND she had a playdate planned that morning – with, according to her friend - her other two daughters. So, how interesting is that the attackers are accusing us of having children who we abandoned for others to raise?

And, par for the course, when I posted a video asking about that phrase, the "other two daughters", the calls started rolling in with people who sound intelligent and articulate who contacted me to say that yes, Christopher Watts' wife did have two other children. I was told that

MISS MENSA'S THEORY ~ on the Case of Christopher Watts Specific to Family Violence and Child Abuse is an opinion essay written to explore whether Christopher Watts is guilty of murdering his wife and their daughters beyond all reasonable doubt.

"everybody in town knows it" and that they also know she gave the children up for adoption.

Do you know why I absolutely believe this is true? Because right from the start every single false accusation the attackers have made against those of us who they are attacking have served to direct us to exactly the sordid details of Christopher Watts' wife's life that isn't quite as pretty as her worshippers are pretending her to be.

It's called projection.

It's called gaslighting.

They throw the accusations out there against us so that when we do discover any of these details about the case then they hope nobody will believe us.

If they can convince others we've filed bankruptcy, then when we say that she did then

MISS MENSA'S THEORY ~ on the Case of Christopher Watts Specific to Family Violence and Child Abuse is an opinion essay written to explore whether Christopher Watts is guilty of murdering his wife and their daughters beyond all reasonable doubt.

the attackers can say well, who are they to say such a thing.

If they can convince others we're lying about our careers or education, when we find out that she was never a nurse – the attackers can say well, who are they to say such a thing.

If they can convince others that we're child abusers and then we find out that it sure does appear to be reasonable to believe that she was medically abusing poor Bella and Ce Ce - then the attackers can say well, who are they to say such a thing.

So, here we are, being accused now of having children who we have given up and now we're hearing that the morning she was "missing' she had a playdate scheduled with HER OTHER TWO DAUGHTERS.

Yes, I believe it. I'm not saying you must believe it too. I'm just telling you my opinion based on what I've seen happening during the last thirteen

MISS MENSA'S THEORY ~ on the Case of Christopher Watts Specific to Family Violence and Child Abuse is an opinion essay written to explore whether Christopher Watts is guilty of murdering his wife and their daughters beyond all reasonable doubt.

months with the organized effort to harm those of us who have been under attack by a group of gangstalking thugs who seem hell-bent on re-creating her "reputation" - by attempting to "destroy" (their word, not mine) the reputations of those of us who they are attacking.

Survivor of Spousal Abuse?

MISS MENSA'S THEORY ~ on the Case of Christopher Watts Specific to Family Violence and Child Abuse is an opinion essay written to explore whether Christopher Watts is guilty of murdering his wife and their daughters beyond all reasonable doubt.

On March 2, 2017, over one year before her death, according to a Facebook post that was emailed to me just the other day, she posted a comment in a "spousal abuse survivor" Facebook group saying that she was in love with another man and that she was scared of the "drastic measures" it would take for her to be with the one she loved.

Some people are saying the Facebook post is a fake. I don't think so. I think the only fake was her.

I think the only fake was the woman who was posting in a spousal abuse survivor Facebook group to begin with when I highly doubt that she was ever a survivor of spousal abuse.

I think the fake was the woman who claimed she earned a car that her husband was on the hook for.

MISS MENSA'S THEORY ~ on the Case of Christopher Watts Specific to Family Violence and Child Abuse is an opinion essay written to explore whether Christopher Watts is guilty of murdering his wife and their daughters beyond all reasonable doubt.

I think the fake was the woman who it sounds like tried to get a dining room table for free.

I think she faked her way all the way through her relationship with Christopher Watts from the day they first met. And he fell for her and he fell for her lies too.

MISS MENSA'S THEORY ~ on the Case of Christopher Watts Specific to Family Violence and Child Abuse is an opinion essay written to explore whether Christopher Watts is guilty of murdering his wife and their daughters beyond all reasonable doubt.

Rain Man?

In my opinion, I think it's possible that Christopher Watts may be on the spectrum. Here is the wiki definition - Asperger syndrome (AS), also known as Asperger's, is a developmental disorder characterized by significant difficulties in social interaction and nonverbal communication, along with restricted and repetitive patterns of behavior and interests.

I think that Christopher Watts was an intelligent and hard-working young man who found his niche with the Nascar training and working as a mechanic. He excelled in school and in sports. He excelled mechanically. He was neat and clean, and he wanted to have everything in order. And he wanted everybody to be happy.

Especially his wife.

MISS MENSA'S THEORY ~ on the Case of Christopher Watts Specific to Family Violence and Child Abuse is an opinion essay written to explore whether Christopher Watts is guilty of murdering his wife and their daughters beyond all reasonable doubt.

I think that Christopher Watts was healthy, active, successful, hard-working, and I think he had formed many life-long healthy relationships with his family members and friends with absolutely no problem at all.

And then he met his wife.

And suddenly, his friends and family members offended her?

He wasn't allowed to go to the gym?

He wasn't allowed to hug his friend's wife?

~

Remember that his co-workers nicknamed him RAIN MAN.

I think Christopher Watts was an easy target for his wife who in my opinion was conning him from the start. And I think he missed the clues.

In fact, I think he missed the obvious.

MISS MENSA'S THEORY ~ on the Case of Christopher Watts Specific to Family Violence and Child Abuse is an opinion essay written to explore whether Christopher Watts is guilty of murdering his wife and their daughters beyond all reasonable doubt.

Were her LIES about to be EXPOSED?

In my opinion, the night that poor little Bella and Ce Ce were murdered, their mother's lies were about to be exposed. They were broke. In fact, I'm surprised that when Christopher Watts took his girlfriend out for a nice salmon dinner that weekend while his wife was in Arizona "on business" - that his bank card worked.

At 2:30 a.m. shortly before she died, Christopher Watts' wife's charge card was denied for an internet purchase of hair care products. Some people talking about the case on social media say that it was an automatic purchase. Others believe that she was probably trying to purchase the hair care products then became livid, or desperate, or both, when she realized her card was tapped out.

MISS MENSA'S THEORY ~ on the Case of Christopher Watts Specific to Family Violence and Child Abuse is an opinion essay written to explore whether Christopher Watts is guilty of murdering his wife and their daughters beyond all reasonable doubt.

Remember, the house payment was due. The kids' daycare center would have been expecting payment the following morning. They were due in court the following week because they were being sued for non-payment of the HOA dues.

To me it appears obvious that she was lying to her husband about just how "successful" she was as a promoter with the MLMs she belonged to.

I think the only reason she ever had any "sales" was because she was using charge cards to buy as much of the product as she needed to buy each month in order to make her "quota". I don't think she was earning any money. And I for damned sure do not believe she was ever making 65k per year.

I think that her husband was leaving her. I think he had already had enough of her crap. I think he was seeing through her façade of success. And I think he was on his way out that door.

The marriage was over.

MISS MENSA'S THEORY ~ on the Case of Christopher Watts Specific to Family Violence and Child Abuse is an opinion essay written to explore whether Christopher Watts is guilty of murdering his wife and their daughters beyond all reasonable doubt.

Her gig was up.

And all her lies were about to be exposed.

If it is true, and again, I do think it's reasonable to believe it is true, that there was an open CPS case against her, what they call a "family plan" to protect Bella and Ce Ce from further medical abuse, then in a divorce she would not have been granted custody of their children.

In a divorce, she would not have received alimony or child support if the children were living with Christopher Watts. In a divorce, she may have been ordered to pay child support, in fact. In a divorce, she would not have been able to afford the house.

In a divorce, her online friends may not have figured it out but anybody who knew her in real-life would have surely noticed that she lost her house, custody of her children, and her income stream too.

MISS MENSA'S THEORY ~ on the Case of Christopher Watts Specific to Family Violence and Child Abuse is an opinion essay written to explore whether Christopher Watts is guilty of murdering his wife and their daughters beyond all reasonable doubt.

I do believe that she realized that her lies were about to be exposed when she finally caught on that their marriage was over.

And in my opinion, she decided to take "drastic measures" to ensure that her secrets would never be found out.

MISS MENSA'S THEORY ~ on the Case of Christopher Watts Specific to Family Violence and Child Abuse is an opinion essay written to explore whether Christopher Watts is guilty of murdering his wife and their daughters beyond all reasonable doubt.

Happy Birthday

In my opinion, Christopher Watts seems to take his social cues from others. He does as he is told. Think about that police interview. He was sitting there acting as if he was trying to please the investigators. He was sitting there not catching on at all to the danger he was in.

Just like in his marriage.

He had no clue how poorly his girlfriend was treating his friends?

He had no clue how poorly his fiancé was treating his family members?

He had no clue how poorly his wife was treating him?

He had no clue they were heading for bankruptcy back in 2015?

MISS MENSA'S THEORY ~ on the Case of Christopher Watts Specific to Family Violence and Child Abuse is an opinion essay written to explore whether Christopher Watts is guilty of murdering his wife and their daughters beyond all reasonable doubt.

He had no clue his wife was in love with another man in 2017? (Based on her Facebook post from March 2, 2017).

He had no clue she stopped making the house payments in December 2017 for the next three months straight?

He had no clue they were already broke again evidently in 2017 and probably even sooner after filing that bankruptcy?

He had no clue she wasn't the huge financial success that she told him she was. In fact, I seriously wonder if he still believes she was a nurse.

He had no clue that the weather does not heal serious diseases.

He had no clue that a woman taking 26 pills a day will not suddenly be able to stop taking her meds.

He had no clue the absurdity of her claim that she took 26 pills per day to begin with.

MISS MENSA'S THEORY ~ on the Case of Christopher Watts Specific to Family Violence and Child Abuse is an opinion essay written to explore whether Christopher Watts is guilty of murdering his wife and their daughters beyond all reasonable doubt.

He had no clue that the Lexus wasn't free after all.

Here is a story about the day to day life of Christopher Watts that might shed some light on their true relationship for you.

Remember that Christopher Watts didn't walk, he ran, when his wife told him to do something, right? He didn't say that he would get to it later. He ran to please her. He ran to do whatever she told him to do and to do it fast, and right, and well.

In one of her videos, she mocked him, as usual, saying that he will do whatever she tells him to do.

She laughed.

But it really wasn't funny.

She had a doormat husband.

MISS MENSA'S THEORY ~ on the Case of Christopher Watts Specific to Family Violence and Child Abuse is an opinion essay written to explore whether Christopher Watts is guilty of murdering his wife and their daughters beyond all reasonable doubt.

And to some of us who are discussing this case on social media, it sure does seem like she was wiping her muddy feet on him every day.

Well, one year on his birthday, there was a celebration going on downstairs while he was upstairs busy trying to get the wet laundry hung up to dry.

One of the attendees wondered where he was and went looking for him while his wife sat at the center of her husband's birthday celebration soaking up the attention.

When he was located upstairs working hard on the laundry, he was asked what he was doing and then encouraged to put his work aside to join the others at his birthday celebration downstairs.

He said that he couldn't.

He said he had to get the laundry hung up just right.

MISS MENSA'S THEORY ~ on the Case of Christopher Watts Specific to Family Violence and Child Abuse is an opinion essay written to explore whether Christopher Watts is guilty of murdering his wife and their daughters beyond all reasonable doubt.

He said that his wife expects him to hang up the children's clothes on the hangers to dry instead of putting their clothes in the dryer.

He was nervous.

He was in a hurry - to get those clothes hung up fast, and to do it right. So, he was doing as he was told. He was doing what he was told to do, exactly as he was told to do it - right away - when she told him it needed to be done – while his sat on her ass, the center of attention, at his birthday celebration.

MISS MENSA'S THEORY ~ on the Case of Christopher Watts Specific to Family Violence and Child Abuse is an opinion essay written to explore whether Christopher Watts is guilty of murdering his wife and their daughters beyond all reasonable doubt.

Was Christopher Watts Actually Telling the Truth When He Said

HE DID NOT MURDER HIS CHILDREN?

In my opinion, Christopher Watts was absolutely telling the truth in his first police interview when he said HE DID NOT MURDER HIS CHILDREN.

In fact, in my opinion, Christopher Watts didn't murder his wife either.

In my opinion, his wife murdered their children then killed herself.

But if I'm right, then why on earth did Christopher Watts plead guilty, right?

I think he pleaded guilty because I don't believe that Christopher Watts is able to stand up for himself.

MISS MENSA'S THEORY ~ on the Case of Christopher Watts Specific to Family Violence and Child Abuse is an opinion essay written to explore whether Christopher Watts is guilty of murdering his wife and their daughters beyond all reasonable doubt.

I think that Christopher Watts was a battered husband.

And I think he was also a high-functioning Aspie who was targeted by his wife from the start to do exactly what she told him to do, when she told him to do it, and how she told him it must be done.

He followed her orders. He did as he was told. He just wanted order and peace and quiet.

He just wanted his wife to be happy.

I think that when he found out his children were murdered, that he closed off into his shell.

And I think that he has yet to emerge as the man he once was before he entered what surely at times, for him and for his family, must have seemed like a marriage from hell.

Did you know that before Christopher Watts flew back to Colorado with his wife and their children that he wrote out and signed a handwritten letter

MISS MENSA'S THEORY ~ on the Case of Christopher Watts Specific to Family Violence and Child Abuse is an opinion essay written to explore whether Christopher Watts is guilty of murdering his wife and their daughters beyond all reasonable doubt.

and left it for safekeeping with his family back home?

That's right - just one week before poor little Bella and Ce Ce were murdered by one of their parents in what should have been the safety of their own home, Christopher Watts sat down at his parents' home in North Carolina and hand wrote a letter which he left behind with his family, just in case...

This is what Christopher Watts wrote just one week before his children were murdered. The letter is dated August 6, 2018 and it reads -

To Whom it May Concern,

If anyone gets this letter, I would never do anything to hurt myself, or my children, or my wife.

If anything happens to me, please investigate my wife.

Chris Watts

MISS MENSA'S THEORY ~ on the Case of Christopher Watts Specific to Family Violence and Child Abuse is an opinion essay written to explore whether Christopher Watts is guilty of murdering his wife and their daughters beyond all reasonable doubt.

Obviously, it appears by his handwritten letter that Christopher Watts was afraid of his wife.

Many years ago, there was a case where the husband called for help, saying that his wife had just committed suicide.

He told the police that his wife had been depressed lately. And that he discovered her dead body which appeared as if she had shot herself.

The police investigated then cleared the scene giving the husband permission to clean and to remove whatever items from his home that he wanted to remove.

He called in his friends from church and they worked hard to clean the house and to remove the bedding that his wife had "committed suicide" on.

MISS MENSA'S THEORY ~ on the Case of Christopher Watts Specific to Family Violence and Child Abuse is an opinion essay written to explore whether Christopher Watts is guilty of murdering his wife and their daughters beyond all reasonable doubt.

Well, a few days later the autopsy was conducted and the authorities learned that, in fact, the wife had suffered TWO FATAL GUNSHOT WOUNDS.

It was determined that it would not have been possible for her to have fired the second shot.

They arrested the husband.

They arrested the husband who thankfully had not found the letter that his wife had written and taped to the underside of the drawer to her china cabinet during his big-time cleaning spree when his friends from church unknowingly helped him dispose of the evidence.

The letter read - in part - that she was not depressed or suicidal - and that if anything happened to her to please investigate her husband.

The letter that Christopher Watts wrote and left behind with his family, in my opinion, speaks volumes for the state their marriage was in.

MISS MENSA'S THEORY ~ on the Case of Christopher Watts Specific to Family Violence and Child Abuse is an opinion essay written to explore whether Christopher Watts is guilty of murdering his wife and their daughters beyond all reasonable doubt.

And as a survivor advocate who has researched family violence for many years and who has earned both my B.A. in psychology and my Juris Doctor with a focus on both family and criminal law, I can say without hesitation that in my opinion, Christopher Watts was a battered husband who was truly in fear for his life.

Consider his interviews from behind bars – he seems at peace, he seems comfortable, he seems secure.

What does that say about his marriage when prison life is comfortable for him?

I do believe that Christopher Watts was a battered husband – and I believe that had he been a battered wife that the case discussion on social media would have been very different.

In fact, I believe that the social justice warriors on social media would have been wanting to hear every last detail of how he was treated instead of the way they have been calling him "guilty", and

MISS MENSA'S THEORY ~ on the Case of Christopher Watts Specific to Family Violence and Child Abuse is an opinion essay written to explore whether Christopher Watts is guilty of murdering his wife and their daughters beyond all reasonable doubt.

"evil" and "a monster" ever since the case first hit the headline news.

I'm not in any way suggesting that ANYBODY deserved to be killed.

What I am suggesting is that the case of Christopher Watts, in my opinion, is one which we should explore, one which we should closely examine, one which we should discuss and learn from – so that hopefully, as a society we gain awareness and are better able to help other children who deserve to be safe in their own home, just like Bella and Ce Ce did too.

If we lock the door and throw away the key without asking the tougher questions and really trying to learn from this case, then we're choosing to ignore the opportunity to learn how to better help other children, and their fathers too, who may be living in a home where dad is running, instead of walking, where dad is missing his own birthday celebration, where dad is delaying taking

MISS MENSA'S THEORY ~ on the Case of Christopher Watts Specific to Family Violence and Child Abuse is an opinion essay written to explore whether Christopher Watts is guilty of murdering his wife and their daughters beyond all reasonable doubt.

his friend to the airport in order to clean the basement because mom told him to, where dad is afraid to let the girls talk to their grandpa because they don't want mom to find out and to get mad, where dad is afraid to speak up because he is afraid his wife will order him out of the house again.

If we choose as a society to ignore this opportunity to study this case closely and to seriously explore the tough issues that the Watts family faced leading up to this tragedy, then we, as a society, are not giving true justice to poor little Bella and Ce Ce.

In my opinion.

What do you think?

Do you think it's possible that Christopher Watts was telling the truth in his police interview when he said that HE DID NOT MURDER HIS CHILDREN?

MISS MENSA'S THEORY ~ on the Case of Christopher Watts Specific to Family Violence and Child Abuse is an opinion essay written to explore whether Christopher Watts is guilty of murdering his wife and their daughters beyond all reasonable doubt.

Try your best to look at this case through a gender-free lens.

Try your best to look at this case with compassion for all parties involved.

Try your best to discuss this case with others while keeping an open mind and only respectful words for each other, whether you agree with somebody else's opinions on the case.

Try your best to examine this case from the eyes of the children.

Take a closer look at the 100s of videos that Christopher Watts' wife posted on social media before her death.

And ask yourself – when you look at Bella – whether you notice the look of both sadness and fear in her eyes.

MISS MENSA'S THEORY ~ on the Case of Christopher Watts Specific to Family Violence and Child Abuse is an opinion essay written to explore whether Christopher Watts is guilty of murdering his wife and their daughters beyond all reasonable doubt.

Afterword

For over ten years straight, I have enjoyed discussing and writing about true crime cases in the headline news specific to family violence and child abuse. And for over ten years straight, I have been able to enjoy this hobby without getting attacked by a group of gangstalking thugs who think they have the right to tell me I am ALLOWED to discuss every other case out there, EXCEPT the case of Christopher Watts.

Well, I don't take kindly to abuse, or to their threats, or to their other criminal acts and the long list of civil infractions they have committed against me.

MISS MENSA'S THEORY ~ on the Case of Christopher Watts Specific to Family Violence and Child Abuse is an opinion essay written to explore whether Christopher Watts is guilty of murdering his wife and their daughters beyond all reasonable doubt.

I will discuss the case of Christopher Watts in the same way that I discuss every other true crime case that I choose to discuss.

Nobody complains when people call Casey Anthony or George Zimmerman guilty, right? Nobody complains when people say O.J. is guilty, right? Nobody complains when people say Steven Avery or Brendan Dassey are innocent, right?

What about Darlie Routier? Nobody complains when people say she's innocent, right?

So, why is it that the attackers think they have the right to attack people for discussing their opinions on the case of Christopher Watts?

Because the attackers are abusers, that's why.

And they are abusers who appear as if they evidently have something to hide.

I will discuss the case of Christopher Watts just like I discuss every other true crime case that piques my interest.

MISS MENSA'S THEORY ~ on the Case of Christopher Watts Specific to Family Violence and Child Abuse is an opinion essay written to explore whether Christopher Watts is guilty of murdering his wife and their daughters beyond all reasonable doubt.

I will offer my opinions on the case.

I will offer my theories on what really happened.

Because by discussing these cases we can gain awareness, as a society, of the issues specific to domestic violence and child abuse.

There is no way to save Bella and Ce Ce.

They were tragically murdered by one of their parents in what should have been the safety of their own home.

But if we can discuss what happened to them, and gain awareness on important issues like the battered husband syndrome, mental illness, the financial dangers of getting involved with product-based MLMs that require monthly purchases, and - in my opinion, the most important issue of all - Munchausen by Proxy - then hopefully we can help protect other children who also deserve - just like Bella and Ce Ce did - to be safe in their own homes - BEFORE it's too late.

MISS MENSA'S THEORY ~ on the Case of Christopher Watts Specific to Family Violence and Child Abuse is an opinion essay written to explore whether Christopher Watts is guilty of murdering his wife and their daughters beyond all reasonable doubt.

About the Author

Brenda Irish Heintzelman is a mom and grandmama' whose greatest joy in life is spending time with her children and grandchildren. She earned her B.A. in Psychology and her Juris Doctor with a focus on both family and criminal law. She is the author of "Safe to Tell" which promotes legislation to provide better legal safeguards for children who are survivors of family violence. Brenda is an avid writer and speaker on the issues of domestic violence and child abuse.

Brenda is a highly skilled Family Court Mediator who is specially trained in child protection. She created the mediator training module titled MIND YOUR MANNERS which she presented at

MISS MENSA'S THEORY ~ on the Case of Christopher Watts Specific to Family Violence and Child Abuse is an opinion essay written to explore whether Christopher Watts is guilty of murdering his wife and their daughters beyond all reasonable doubt.

the annual bar association ADR conference which is designed to help mediators promote effective communication between parents taking part in the mediation process and to keep their focus on what matters most – the best interests of their children.

In addition to owning her own mediation practice, Brenda is a real estate broker with 20 years of experience helping families buy and sell residential real estate and she has also been a firearms instructor and range officer since 2010.

MISS MENSA'S THEORY ~ on the Case of Christopher Watts Specific to Family Violence and Child Abuse is an opinion essay written to explore whether Christopher Watts is guilty of murdering his wife and their daughters beyond all reasonable doubt.

Printed in Great Britain
by Amazon